Past Lives, Present Miracles

❖ ALSO BY DENISE LINN ❖

Books/Oracle Cards

Altars: Bringing Sacred Shrines into Your Everyday Life

Dream Lover: Using Your Dreams to Enhance Love in Your Life

Feng Shui for the Soul: How to Create a Harmonious
Environment That Will Nurture and Sustain You*

Four Acts of Personal Power:
How to Heal Your Past and Create a Positive Future*

The Hidden Power of Dreams:
The Mysterious World of Dreams Revealed*

If I Can Forgive, So Can You: My Autobiography of How I
Overcame My Past and Healed My Life*

The Mystic Cookbook: The Secret Alchemy of Food
(with Meadow Linn)*

Quest: A Guide for Creating Your Own Vision Quest
(with Meadow Linn)*

Sacred Space: Clearing and Enhancing the Energy of Your Home

The Secret Language of Signs: How to Interpret the
Coincidences and Symbols in Your Life

Secrets & Mysteries: The Glory and Pleasure of Being a Woman*

Soul Coaching®: 28 Days to Discover Your Authentic Self*

Soul Coaching® Oracle Cards: What Your Soul Wants You to
Know (a 52-card deck and guidebook)*

The Soul Loves the Truth: Lessons Learned on My Path to Joy*

Space Clearing: How to Purify and Create
Harmony in Your Home

Space Clearing A–Z: How to Use Feng Shui to
Purify and Bless Your Home*

Unlock the Secret Messages of Your Body! A 28-Day Jump-
Start Program for Radiant Health and Glorious Vitality*

Audio Programs

Angels! Angels! Angels!
Cellular Regeneration: How to Heal
Complete Relaxation*
Dreams
Journeys into Past Lives*
Life Force: Access the Energy Field Around You
Past Lives and Beyond
Phoenix Rising: Rising above Limitations
33 Spirit Journeys*
The Way of the Drum

Video

Instinctive Feng Shui for Creating Sacred Space:
How to Cleanse and Harmonize the Energy in Your Home*

*Available from Hay House

Please visit Hay House USA: **www.hayhouse.com**®
Hay House Australia: **www.hayhouse.com.au**
Hay House UK: **www.hayhouse.co.uk**
Hay House South Africa: **www.hayhouse.co.za**
Hay House India: **www.hayhouse.co.in**

Past Lives, Present Miracles

Denise Linn

HAY HOUSE, INC.
Carlsbad, California • New York City
London • Sydney • Johannesburg
Vancouver • Hong Kong • New Delhi

Published and distributed in the United States by: Hay House, Inc.: www
.hayhouse.com • **Published and distributed in Australia by:** Hay House
Australia Pty. Ltd.: www.hayhouse.com.au • **Published and distributed
in the United Kingdom by:** Hay House UK, Ltd.: www.hayhouse.co.uk •
Published and distributed in the Republic of South Africa by: Hay House
SA (Pty), Ltd.: www.hayhouse.co.za • **Distributed in Canada by:** Raincoast
Books: www.raincoast.com • **Published in India by:** Hay House Publishers
India: www.hayhouse.co.in

Editorial supervision: Jill Kramer • *Interior design:* Tricia Breidenthal
Cover design: Louis Zimmerman

Originally published in 1997 in the U.S. by Ballantine and by Piatkus Books
in the UK under the title *Past Lives, Present Dreams.*

Library of Congress Cataloging-in-Publication Data

Linn, Denise.
  Past lives, present miracles / Denise Linn.
    p. cm.
  ISBN 978-1-4019-1682-4 (tradepaper)
  1. Reincarnation. 2. Self-actualization (Psychology) 3. Reincarnation
therapy. I. Title.
  BP573.R5L56 2008
  133.901'35--dc22
                                                2007038656

ISBN: 978-1-4019-1682-4

17 16 15 14   9 8 7 6
1st Hay House edition, March 2008

Printed in the United States of America

To my husband, David,
and my daughter, Meadow . . .
fellow travelers through time and space.

CONTENTS

Preface: The Time Is Now! xi

Introduction: About This Book xix

Chapter 1:   My Journey into Past Lives 1

Chapter 2:   Reincarnation and Karma 35

Chapter 3:   How Past-Life Exploration
Can Heal Your Life 57

Chapter 4:   Tracking Clues . . .
Becoming a Past-Life Detective 85

Chapter 5:   Past-Life Clues Questionnaire 121

Chapter 6:   Regression . . . a Journey of
Transformation 157

Chapter 7:   Dreams and Past Lives 181

Chapter 8:   Resolution: How to Heal Past-Life
Blockages During Regression 203

Chapter 9:   Spirit Guides, Angels, and Past Lives 221

Chapter 10:   Future Lives, the Ripple Effect,
and Miracles 253

Afterword: Time, Space, and Beyond: The Next Step 269

Acknowledgments 273

About the Author 275

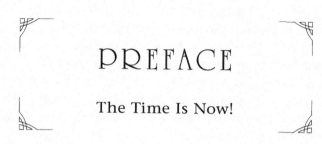

PREFACE

The Time Is Now!

Miracles can occur in your life easily and effortlessly. It's simply a matter of remembering who you are—and in order to do this, you must clear the blockages that stand between you and your soul. Almost all of these obstacles have their roots in your far past, so it's immensely valuable to travel back into time to release them. However, most of us are so caught up in limiting beliefs about who we are and what we deserve that it's almost impossible to take that journey. This book can show you how.

If you really want to know who you are, and you're ready for miracles to blossom in your life, *Past Lives, Present Miracles* will reveal secret pathways that will help you clear your inner clutter so that you can truly discover why you're here. With this knowledge, you'll learn how to manifest your innermost dreams. The time is now! You wouldn't be holding this book in your hands if you weren't prepared to begin the journey.

Why Now?

It's an exciting time to be alive. In fact, there has never been a more powerful time to move beyond personal limitations and step off the karmic treadmill toward your maximum potential. It's only now, after eons of evolutionary cycles, that you truly have the ability to come full circle into the blueprint of your soul. As our planet has entered into a new millennium and vibration, you can finally resolve old issues that originated in your past lives . . . and as a result, miracles will abound!

My teacher Dancing Feather, from the Taos Pueblo in New Mexico, planted the seeds for this book many years ago. He was humble, yet he carried great wisdom within himself. Although we are of different tribes, this serene old man helped me connect more profoundly to my Cherokee heritage, as he shared prophecies for our time and talked about the importance of releasing shadows from the past.

I remember being with him one warm summer evening. Wearing a faded cowboy shirt and well-worn jeans, he sat cross-legged on the wild grasses of the sun-baked high mesa. As a soft breeze rustled dried leaves and scattered them around us, I strained to hear his voice. His skin seemed to glow as it reflected the crimson sunset. Deep age lines were etched into his face and his once jet-black hair was now salt-and-pepper, yet when he spoke he had an animated, childlike humility. Sometimes when he was talking, he'd stop and stare into the distance. His eyes, clouded over with age, seemed to peer into an inner world. After a moment, he'd continue to speak again.

A New Cycle Is Beginning

Dancing Feather told me that Mother Earth was at the end of a long cycle—a time of completion and rebirth—and huge changes were going to occur in the fabric of our lives. He said that the renewal would be difficult for many people because they were lost; that is, they were missing the connection to their roots and didn't know who they were. They were unable to find themselves in each and every part of nature. My gentle teacher said that human beings weren't separate from the mountains, the vast sky, the meadows, and the seas . . . we were part of all things, great and small. Unfortunately, some had forgotten this.

He talked about the significance of our dreams and the fact that our nocturnal journeys are an entrance point into the inner realms. In the years ahead, he said, they'd be a valuable source of inspiration and healing and would play an increasingly important role in our collective evolution. He also explained that it's essential to release the shadows of pain, suffering, and wounds from the past, as they keep us from fully experiencing the beauty around us. We must learn to listen to our inner wisdom and to the spirit ancestors and guides around us. In order to remember who we truly are, *we have to reach for the stars.*

My teacher also spoke excitedly about the great potential for us in the time ahead. Although he didn't speak specifically of past lives, he did discuss the need for inner and outer purification, and the necessity to heal ancient wounds.

Since the years following Dancing Feather's death, I've seen the wisdom of his words. Our planet is indeed rapidly transforming—just as he'd prophesied. Tremendous changes in technology and our natural resources are taking place, which is affecting the way we relate to one another and our environment. As a culture, for the most part we've forgotten that everything on our planet is connected, linking us all to a living universe that's no less alive than a majestic whale in the sea or an expanse of wildflowers on a hillside. We've forgotten that our world sings with life and vibrates with the intensity of Spirit.

Global Purification

The way the universe responds to planetary imbalances can be compared to the way our bodies respond to injury. When we suffer damage, our body responds by sending healing energy to the site of the distress. We're not aware of the myriad biochemical processes that occur in the body's immune system; however, when we're hurt, the body automatically reacts—it's a natural response.

The human body is a microcosm of the universe; in other words, our planet can be likened to one cell in the body of the living universe. And right now, our planet is injured and *we're all being affected by this*. The universe is sending healing energy to us, just the way the human immune system becomes activated when it detects an injury. As waves of healing energy infiltrate our planet, a massive purification is beginning to take place, which is causing a cosmic stirring up of old structures and institutions and limiting beliefs.

Global purification is similar to the cleansing of a deep, stagnant pond. The top six inches of the pond may appear clear, but below the surface it's choked with silt and unhealthy growth. When there's a sudden infusion of fresh clear water from springs surging below, all the fetid water is churned upward. The short-term effects seem chaotic, as the pond actually looks worse—it's muddy and foul with decaying matter. However, the purification process is essential for the health of the pond, which soon becomes crystal clear and sweet. Today our planet isn't unlike the stagnant pond: The new frequencies that are emerging are like rejuvenating springs that cause upheaval as they initiate incredible cleansing and healing.

Personal Purification and Renewal

As we face the exciting and challenging times ahead, we have the enormous potential to release the heavy burdens we've each carried within us for lifetime after lifetime. The cosmic stirring up of old structures and hierarchies means that ancient blockages are currently surfacing. As new energies flood the planet, people are experiencing an intense resurgence of past issues, which results in temporary feelings of disorientation and turmoil. Many individuals are dealing with—and resolving—their grief, fear, and rage over these situations, which had been previously buried deep within or denied.

But the suppression of pain and suffering in this life, *as well as in previous lives,* is now coming to light, as many people are struggling to overcome their barriers to wholeness. All of the pain of our separation from Spirit that has accrued within us over countless lifetimes—and exists inside us as suppressed memories—is crying for release. Unlike any other time in the history of our planet, we now have the opportunity to truly let go of these old limitations from the past.

Deep within each of us is a vast, interconnected universe where the past, present, and future swirl in a great orchestration of light and sound. It's the dwelling place of the soul—the place within us that's authentic and true. It's infinite and eternal . . . and never changes through a multitude of incarnations. As we've entered a new millennium, the veil between the inner universes and the outer one around us is thinning. We have the ability to step into the mysterious realms of self and see the inner truths that have been hidden from us for so long.

There are many shadows that present themselves in life: fear, low self-esteem, anger, sadness, poverty, loneliness, self-limiting beliefs, disease, and death. They almost always have their source in past lives. The challenge, in the years to come, is to face your shadows and see who you've been in past lives so that you can live more richly in the present. But the journey beyond the darkness requires the willingness to take risks—and only those who risk will truly live.

The odyssey ahead also invites you to step into the grace of forgiveness—to be willing to forgive what you've done to others in the past, as well as to forgive what others have done to you both in this life and beyond. True forgiveness is the capacity to accept the reality of another . . . and to do so is an act of power. *The time is now.* The journey into your past lives can be a turning point and can uncover your deepest levels of compassion and transformation.

The processes described in this book will activate a sacred journey of the soul, and once you've chosen that path, you may not return. However, it's a passageway that, once taken, will create miracles in your life and enhance your ability to experience powerful depths of love—love for yourself, others, and the planet. It's a path that will help you make a difference in the world.

INTRODUCTION

About This Book

As the transformation of our planet intensifies, exploring past lives can be an increasing source of healing and inspiration. But how can you best take advantage of the energies now available for growth and personal expansion? In what ways can you remember who you were in your former lives and then release any negative programming that has carried forward into your present life? How does releasing blockages from the past help you create miracles in your current existence? What should you do so that you can remember your dreams and understand what they're trying to tell you? Why is this a very significant time in history? In the following chapters, I'll give you the simple, viable answers and solutions.

This book offers easy-to-use techniques to help you recall events from your previous lives. It also explains reincarnation and karma, and why these concepts are so important at this time. You'll learn how to use *past-life clues* to discover who you were in earlier incarnations. In the pages to come, you'll find specific methods to release persistent conditions such as current fears and phobias, physical ailments, relationship difficulties, and blockages to abundance and creativity. In addition, you'll read about your spirit guides and explore exercises that will enable you to contact them.

As our planet's vibratory rate continues to accelerate, it's vital that you listen to the secrets of your soul. I'll teach you how to program, remember, and interpret these messages.

Examples of past-life regressions are presented throughout this work—some of them are from my clients, while others are from letters I've received or conversations I've had with people who have attended my past-life seminars. In some cases, I've quoted exactly from the letters, but when I've paraphrased or shortened the description for easier reading, I've tried to maintain the spirit of the person's experience as much as possible. For some stories, I've changed the names of people in order to protect the privacy of the individuals involved.

Right now in our human evolution, massive, exciting changes that have been foretold by native cultures around the world are beginning to occur on many levels. The aim of this book is to provide you with information and techniques that will show you how to release the past so that you can manifest miracles, experience joy in your everyday life, and prepare for upcoming events.

We are the spiritual heirs of the planet. If we can let go of the ancient blockages and limitations from the past and listen to the inner guidance of our soul, we can lovingly step into the future.

Chapter One

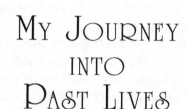

My Journey into Past Lives

My journey into the mysterious world of past lives began very dramatically in the summer of 1967, when I was 17 years old. I was riding my motorbike on a country road in our small farming community in the Midwest. It was a hazy, peaceful day. My hair was blowing in the wind as I drove past lush cornfields.

Abruptly, my serenity was shattered as a car rear-ended me, throwing me violently to the ground. As I struggled to my feet, I saw a man pointing a gun at me. The dark barrel of the gun seemed enormous. I had no idea who he was. I hadn't done anything to him . . . and I didn't know why he was doing this to me.

Just before he pulled the trigger, a thought raced across my mind: *He's aiming too low.* The sound was explosive as he shot me, and eventually I was left bleeding on the side of the road. A salesman driving by found me and called an ambulance.

In the emergency room, the lights were harsh and bright. Sharp pain stabbed through me, and shrill voices seemed to echo in my brain. I heard people shouting in horror, "She's been shot!"

Then slowly, the lights began to dim and the pain subsided. I felt myself slip into a comfortable, soft blackness where I rested in a bubble-like cocoon. It was at this point, I was told later, that the doctors thought I had died.

Suddenly, the bubble seemed to burst, and I was bathed in a golden light. In fact, I wasn't just enveloped in light—I *was* the light. It was strange that this didn't seem unusual to me; it felt completely normal. I then became aware of unbelievably sweet and pure music. Sound waves and light flowed through me until I actually felt like I *became* the music and the luminescence. I was made of nothing but fluid light and sound. Although this may sound strange, the light and sound weren't separate from each other, but merged together as one. Yet it didn't seem at all odd to me in that moment.

I had no sense of the passing of time. Everything existed *now,* and the past—and the future—was inconceivable. It was as difficult to imagine linear time *there* as it is for me to experience nonlinear time *here.* Everything just *was,* and it didn't seem peculiar at all. I was also overwhelmed by a deep sense of familiarity. I knew I'd been there before—many times. It was the most real thing that I'd ever gone through. Everything else was an illusion.

Infused into this experience was a wonderful kind of love that was as natural as breathing. It was infinite like the universe itself, penetrating every aspect of me. I absolutely knew that it was the only true thing that ever existed. The word *God* doesn't even begin to convey the vast, yet intimate, love I experienced.

Immersed in that exquisite feeling, I wasn't alone. You were there, too—in fact, there wasn't anyone or anything that *wasn't* there. We were all there—without bounds and without separation. I was everyone, and everyone was me; I was you and you were me. We were all one, yet at the same time, we each appeared to be individual. I can't find the words to describe this, and I know this doesn't sound possible . . . yet it was true.

Feeling no longer confined to my body, I experienced boundlessness and a sense of unity with all of life—I was ecstatic to be back in my true home. I saw a great river of glistening golden light before me. As I looked to the far shore, I knew that when I reached it, I'd never return to my 17-year-old body. I'd never been happier as I stepped into the river, but when I was halfway across, a deep and powerful voice boomed: "You may not stay here. There's something you still need to do."

But even as my mind screamed *No!* it felt like I'd been lassoed and was being dragged back to my physical body.

I woke up in my hospital bed. Day after day I fought for my life, struggling not only with physical pain but also with tremendous grief over returning to my body. I didn't want to be on Earth. I wanted to go back to the light. It was the worst homesickness that you could imagine.

Every evening, however, I experienced a miracle. After the lights were turned down and I was alone, I'd close my eyes and feel a hand slip gently into mine, as a wonderful feeling of comfort and safety flooded my being. The first time this happened I was shocked, because when I opened my eyes to see who had come into the room, I couldn't *see* the hand that held mine, but I could *feel* the contours of fingers and palm and the warmth it radiated. Sometimes the hand would release mine, and a different hand would lovingly slide into its place. I particularly remember a very small childlike hand comforting me one night. I knew I was safe and wasn't alone. I believe those hands belonged to my spirit guardians.

The doctors thought I wouldn't survive. My body was severely traumatized after being hit by the car; and the bullet had gone through my spine and damaged a lung after tearing away my spleen, an adrenal gland, and injuring my stomach and intestines. Eventually one of my kidneys was removed and a plastic tube was inserted into my heart to replace my aorta. In addition to being told that I'd most likely be an invalid my entire life (and not to expect to live very long), I was also told that I'd never be able to have children.

However, during those few minutes when the doctors thought I was dead, my consciousness shifted and this changed the course of my life forever. The doctors' dire prognosis didn't matter because a healing ability within me had been activated, and I knew that I'd survive. In those mysterious and magical moments beyond death's door, part of my previous identity was altered, allowing for my survival and rapid recovery. This transformation made it much easier to heal. When I realized that my body wasn't "me"—it was just something that part of me inhabited—I had many more resources to heal myself with than just those available to my physical body. As a result of my new awareness, I recovered very quickly and was out of the hospital in just a few weeks. The doctors called it a miracle; however, I knew that it was due to a change of consciousness.

A Transformed Life . . . the Past, Present, and Future Aren't Sequential

After my near-death experience, my sense of self was completely different. After I was shot, I no longer believed that when my body died, *I* died. I knew that life was eternal and my existence didn't begin at conception and end at death. I no longer felt separate from everything and everyone else on the planet. Time wasn't linear, nor was the universe governed by fixed rules of physics. The evolution in my consciousness forever changed my beliefs about the nature of reality.

As a result of what I experienced on the other side, I realized that from a spiritual perspective, our past, present, and future lives aren't sequential . . . but are all occurring at the same time. However, because we're linear beings and experience everything in terms of past, present, and future, our lives seem as if they occur in a chronological manner.

To help you understand this idea of concurrent lives, imagine a multifaceted mirrored ball hanging above a circular ballroom and radiating reflections throughout the room. As the ball moves, the individual reflections move, too. Pick one reflection and place your awareness on it. Imagine that the reflection you've focused upon represents your current life.

5

You appear to be moving forward. The scenes around you are changing, as you seem to be steadily progressing through time. There are other reflections in front of you and behind you. The ones that are trailing you—as you move around the room—can be thought of as your past lives. They give the impression of *past* lives because they're seemingly in back of you. Those that are ahead of you are your future lives. They appear to be moving through time as well.

The distances between the reflections seem to stay constant—perhaps two feet between you and the closest reflection behind you, and three feet between you and the reflection in front. Given that you're in a perfectly round room, those distances won't change even though the mirrored ball is moving. This gives credence to the illusion that time is fixed—no matter where your reflection has traveled in the ballroom, there's always two feet between you and the nearest reflection behind you and three feet in front. This is measurable and constant.

Looking at this in terms of past and future lives, if one foot is equal to 100 years, then it might seem that there are 200 years between your current life and your most recent past life, and 300 years between your present life and your next life. However, as you move up the beam of light toward the mirrored ball (which is the source of your reflection), the closest reflections in front of and behind you change, and the distances become much shorter. This demonstrates how the separation between past, present, and future is diminishing. The more we collectively move toward our Source, the more our perceptions of time and space will begin to change. The closer you move to the Source, the more difficult it will be to discern the boundaries between past, present, and future.

Here's another way to perceive the thinning of the boundaries of time: Imagine that you left your individual mirrored-ball reflection and traveled "forward in time" around the circumference of the circular room. Eventually you'd come full circle and reach your past lives. Likewise, if you traveled "backward in time," you'd soon complete the circle and reach your future lives.

All the reflections on the ballroom wall seem separate and individual. Some of the reflections are future or past lives, and some can be thought of as other people's lives. However, if you traveled from your individual reflection to the Source (the mirrored ball), you'd see that all lives—past, present, and future—all people, and all matter are resonating from the same Source. We're not separate from anyone else, nor are we separate from what we call the *past* and the *future*. All lives are coexisting, intertwined and dependent upon each other right now. (*Please note:* In this book I talk about our past lives as if they're sequential because this is the way we experience time in our collective reality as human beings.)

The Radiant Light and Sound of the World

Although seemingly the world around me was the same after I got out of the hospital, my experience of it was completely different. Every moment was full of color, sound, and vibrant energy. Each blade of grass glowed in its own light, singing its own song. (As bizarre as it sounds, I could actually hear tones coming out of the grass.) An entire field of wild grass was like a great orchestra of radiant light and shimmering music! Trees had a deep, sonorous hum; and when their leaves fluttered in the wind, it sounded like beautiful crystalline chimes. Even the earth beneath my bare feet pulsed with the cadence of life—I could feel and hear its rhythm. I began to see colors and light around people and everything else (which are called auras, I later learned). And I heard wonderful music that no one else seemed to hear. I had great difficulty understanding that most people couldn't feel and see this overwhelming beauty around them. I couldn't comprehend cruelty or violence because I knew that we were part of one huge, vibrant, living universe . . . and that we couldn't hurt others without hurting ourselves.

As a result of my near-death experience, I've realized that we are infinite and eternal; and we are all intimately connected—cosmically linked, so to speak. I can't truly get home until you do, and vice versa. I also believe that time is malleable so that we can change the past as well as the future. I now have faith in God, angels, and guides. I know we have all experienced past lives, and we all have an innate ability to create the universe around us. In fact, we're subconsciously creating it right now through our thoughts, feelings, and the core beliefs we've carried forward from other lifetimes.

Near Death . . . Touching the Light

Thousands of people have had experiences similar to mine, and certain elements are common in most of them. The initial stages of the near-death experience usually involve sensations of deep peace and of being unattached to the body or of floating above it. Many feel as if they were sucked into a tunnel with a light at the far end of it where they were greeted by beings of light or by individuals they'd known but who'd already died. In almost all cases, these people felt very loved and cared for. Often during this experience, individuals are given the opportunity to review their lives from an observer's point of view. They almost always feel that they hadn't completed what they needed to do on Earth, yet there's a tremendous reluctance to return to the physical body.

Research has shown that those who've had such experiences share similar traits, and in almost all cases, they've been changed by the event. They tend to fear death much less than most people do. On the whole, they feel a greater sense of inner peace and zest for living. In addition, they're often drawn toward the caring professions.

Having a near-death experience doesn't make me special. I think that in my case, I was so far off my spiritual path that it took a cosmic kick to get me back on track. I believe the universe is always whispering to us, and if we don't listen to the whispers, we'll hear the screams. Being attacked was like a huge shout from Spirit: "Denise, remember who you are!"

That shout continues to echo in my life. I came back with the knowledge that this is the most important time in the evolution of our planet. I now realize that the growth—individually and collectively—of our consciousness is essential for the future of our world. I also developed a deep desire to understand life in light of the past lives that we've lived, and I learned that knowledge of past lives could open the door to deep personal healing. I know now that we're never alone; there are always spirit guides and helpers around us, pouring out their love and wisdom. I also awakened to an awareness of the immense potential available to each of us within our dreams, and that dreams can be an avenue to travel back to Spirit. My life became a quest to remember who I am, and my explorations into past lives have helped me along that path.

The Door to My Dreams

After my near-death experience, not only was I set on a spiritual quest to understand the inner nature of time and space, but also the door to my dreams immediately flew open. Vivid and sometimes disturbing images flooded into me during the night. At times these images seemed so real that the boundaries between waking and sleeping hours were blurred. Some dreams were idyllic and even visionary in nature. These dreams were profoundly soothing and reassuring, and occasionally I'd even catch a fleeting glimpse of the place I'd traveled to the moment the doctors thought I'd died. I'd clutch at these cloudy images, only to have them vanish like fine mist.

Often, however, my dreams were disturbing. As the nocturnal doors of perception opened for me, I saw images that had been held back for a long time. Numerous visages of past lifetimes, seemingly forgotten in the recesses of my mind, began to surge forward, allowing me to experience other eras and places in history. The onslaught of these pictures filling my night hours can be likened to a computer downloading information or to a dam whose walls have held back a great river for many years but have finally broken. Through my dreams, I began to understand that so many of my beliefs about myself and the world came from other lifetimes. By recalling these memories, I was bringing into my consciousness old, limiting beliefs, decisions, and judgments that I'd carried through lifetime after lifetime. Now I could begin to release them.

There's a psychological adage that says, "To relive is to relieve," and it seemed that these dream images were helping me relive forgotten experiences so that I could begin to relieve the burden that the past was holding over my current life. By exploring my previous lives in my dreams, as well as using other techniques, I began to heal—physically and emotionally.

My Journey into Healing

As a result of being shot, my youthful ambition to become a scientist was replaced by a yearning to discover why we're here and what our human destiny is. Eventually, I moved into a Zen Buddhist monastery, where I lived for more than two years. I didn't experience any great enlightenment, as I'd hoped, but I did discover a place of stillness inside me in the silence between my thoughts.

As I mentioned, many people who have near-death experiences become healers, and I also found myself drawn into the healing fields. Conventional medical practitioners had told me that due to the severity of my injuries, I'd be disabled for the rest of what would be a short life. But I instinctively knew that I could heal my body—without their kind of medicine.

My spiritual journey toward health and healing first led me to a Hawaiian *kahuna* (shaman), Morna Simeona, who agreed to train me only after discovering that I was of Native American heritage. (My mother is of Cherokee ancestry.) Morna helped me see, even more deeply, that the Spirit resides in everything. She showed me that life isn't always what it seems, and there truly is magic in the universe.

I was also led to a remarkable Japanese woman named Hawayo Takata, the Grand Master of Reiki who brought this ancient practice from the Japanese monasteries to the United States. (Reiki is a method of channeling healing energy.) When we first met, she announced that she knew I was coming because she had seen me in her meditations. She'd been waiting more than a year for me to contact her, and in an almost terse way, she asked what had taken me so long. (She'd wanted me to organize her first courses for Westerners, which I eventually did.) Takata Sensei, who was not only my teacher but who also became a good friend, taught me how to access the life-force energy in such a way that it would surge down into my arms in order for me to offer Reiki healing to others.

I also trained with a shiatsu master, from whom I learned to balance the body by putting pressure on various points that are similar to those used in acupuncture, and I eventually taught shiatsu throughout the world.

As I healed myself from my injuries, people came to me and asked if I could help them heal as well. My practice had developed very quickly, and I discovered that I had a natural ability to channel healing energy through my hands. The results were remarkable and I had more clients than I could possibly schedule.

When a patient would come to me for a first treatment, I'd ask him or her to lie flat on a massage table or futon, and I'd become very still. My breathing would slow down, and I'd wait until I felt a warm breeze of energy fill my body. My hands would become really warm—almost hot—and I'd place them softly on the patient's head until I felt a stream of energy within me begin to flow into the person I was treating.

Next, I'd begin pushing pressure points on the body; each point corresponds with a different organ or gland. As I'd apply pressure, I'd often feel as though I were disappearing into the point—each one seemed like it was a tunnel to the stars . . . and the universe. The patient would seem to disappear. I'd disappear, too. There were only stars, light, and harmonious sound.

Just as every blade of grass and every leaf had light emanating from it and had a unique sound, I found that each shiatsu point had a different tone and color that changed according to the client's health. As I explored my patients' remarkable inner universes, I saw that each point also had a special harmonic or subfrequency, forming a connection with an infinity of inner universes.

Every acupressure point that I pushed not only balanced the organs of the physical body, but it also reached into the innermost places of the patient's being, which created an outward ripple. I knew that in the stillness of my healing room, the world was a better place because of what we were doing. Healing energy was radiating from each pressure point on the body to a corresponding power point on the planet and into the universe. It felt like each point synchronized both healer and patient with the primordial rhythm of the galaxy. In those healing sessions, I felt very close to the infinite light and love that I'd felt in my near-death experience.

All Healing Is Self-Healing

The most powerful healing came when I entered into a place where the boundaries between my client and myself diminished—where I wasn't the healer, nor was the other person the patient. With each treatment, not only did my patients greatly benefit, but I was further healed as well. I began to realize that all my healing work on others was essentially self-fulfilling. Each patient was a part of my greater self—that part of each of us that dwells in all people and things. Each of my patients was a different aspect of myself and represented a particular part of me that needed help.

For example, at one point a number of cancer patients came for treatment. As I worked with them, I realized that there were a number of similarities between us. Their disease was eating away at them, and even though I didn't have a physical illness, I had emotional issues that were slowly consuming me. These issues transformed spontaneously at the same time that my patients experienced positive results from their sessions. I realized that the healing process always began with me. I was never really healing anyone but myself. Working in this way with clients was remarkable, and I was often booked a year in advance because of profound results that my clients achieved.

My Journey into Leading Past-Life Regressions

In my hands-on healing practice, I usually had excellent results. Every once in a while, however, I'd work with someone whose physical or emotional pain would leave for a time but would return later. This was frustrating to me. Realizing that many of our current problems have their source in the past, I began to regress patients to earlier incidents in their lives—oftentimes back to childhood.

I'd usually use relaxation techniques to start these regressions. I'd ask my patients to lie down and relax, and then I'd help them with breathing methods and visualization processes. I'd then suggest that they remember an incident from the day before. After they'd relive this memory, I'd suggest remembering an incident from the previous week, then the previous month, and I'd continue taking them back in time until they'd arrive at early childhood. In this way, my patients were able to recall buried negative beliefs that they'd formed during those years.

I found that many present-day problems could be healed by regressing to early childhood—and then releasing the limiting decisions and beliefs that originated there. For example, a man with a sore shoulder came to me for hands-on treatment. After I worked on him, his shoulder was fine. However, the pain returned three weeks later, so I regressed him to a time in his childhood in which he spontaneously remembered that his father had struck him on the shoulder because he thought that he wasn't meeting his responsibilities. Now as a grown man, my patient believed he wasn't being responsible enough. He subconsciously associated feeling irresponsible with having soreness in his shoulder. So whenever he felt irresponsible, he unconsciously re-created the pain.

We subconsciously manifest situations in the present that are similar to those in the past. We also restimulate the repressed experiences from the past so that we can release them. When my patient regressed to his childhood, he was able to release the grief, pain, and anger that he'd suppressed at the time his father struck him. By surrendering those feelings, the pain in his shoulder eased and didn't return.

As children, we've all made decisions about life that have continued to influence us as adults. I discovered that helping people regress to the time in their lives when vital negative decisions were made could, more often that not, release those decisions and the corresponding symptoms *forever.*

Poisoned in India

There were a few persistent cases, however, when even after a regression to childhood, the symptoms returned. I was very puzzled by this. My client Janet had suffered from ulcers for years. Her doctor had prescribed drugs, a change in her diet, and participation in stress-reduction classes. Despite this, the ulcers persisted. Acting on intuition, she came to me for a treatment. We decided that we might find some clues to her condition in her early childhood. She regressed to the ages of 12, 10, 7, and 6 . . . then suddenly became distressed and began to hyperventilate. I told her to watch the childhood circumstances calmly and then asked what she was experiencing.

"I've been poisoned!" she cried.

"When you were six, you had some poison?" I asked.

"No! I've been poisoned!" she insisted. (I was concerned, thinking that we uncovered a childhood memory of someone deliberately giving her poison.)

I asked, "Who's poisoning you?"

"Enemies of my husband are forcing me to take poison."

"Where are you?" I asked, knowing that she wasn't currently married.

"I'm in India."

At my prompting, Janet proceeded to tell me that she was the young wife of an older man whose strong political beliefs were in opposition to those in power. She described the anguish she experienced. Although she loved her husband and wanted to support him, at the same time, she didn't like the disharmony that his beliefs were causing in their life. One night when her husband was away, his enemies broke into their house and forced her to drink poison. She died feeling helpless and powerless.

I asked her to go back in time into the life that she was seeing and replay it—this time making decisions that would help her feel more in charge of her life and destiny. She did so and saw herself actively campaigning to get other people in the village to understand her husband's point of view. She saw people rallying around her husband so that he had a firm platform of support, which provided strength and protection. She saw herself and her husband raising a family, living a long and happy life, and then dying at an old age—well loved in the community. As she described this revised scene, her entire countenance changed and her face shone with a deep peace.

After this session we talked about her present life. She was in a relationship in which she felt helpless, and the ulcers had started around the same time that she'd entered into it. We discussed some choices she could make, and within a few weeks, the ulcers had healed completely and didn't return.

Janet's present relationship difficulties had activated memories of similar problems in her past life. In her subconscious, she had equated feeling helpless with poison burning holes in her stomach. Feeling impotent in her current life activated the past-life physical trauma, so she manifested ulcers that caused a burning sensation in her stomach. By altering the images in her subconscious, she was able to change negative programming that was affecting her life now.

When I saw the results in Janet's life, I was very excited by the potential of past-life regression. Dealing with problems only in the present can be likened to mowing dandelions. You can cut them down, but they'll keep popping up again and again. It's only by digging down into the roots that you can prevent them from resurfacing. In my healing practice, when I found a problem that couldn't be solved by hands-on healing, shiatsu, massage, or exploring one's early childhood, I'd regress the patient to the roots of the problem in a former life. After resolving the past-life issues, the symptoms would almost always permanently disappear.

I found that most of our present blockages can be traced back to a past life, and by experiencing what occurred in the past, we can heal current-day physical and emotional problems. With past-life regression, my patients released ailments and phobias, mended relationship difficulties, increased their creativity, and released blockages to abundance. The results were amazing.

Pressure Points as Secret Channels to Past Lives

Later I discovered another technique for tuning in to past lives. When I pushed on a shiatsu point with my thumbs, I began to see images in my mind. Likewise, the person whom I was working on would often spontaneously see the same images in his or her mind. Sometimes these "memories" were from early childhood that had been forgotten, but more often they were snapshots of past lives that my client had experienced. Indeed, every point seemed to be a sacred tunnel into the far past.

I realized that past-life memories are lodged not only in the brain but also in the body, and stimulating those images for recall had enormous positive results in my patients' lives. I believe that every cell in the body has consciousness, and each cell holds emotions and past-life memories. Just as DNA has a blueprint for the physical body encoded into its structure, within its intricate makeup are also memories from this life *and past lives!* This was an important discovery for the work that I was to do later with group past-life regressions, in which I got people to stimulate points on their bodies in order to help facilitate past-life recall.

Many of my clients began to report that after my treatments, their dreams began to change, often featuring images and memories of other times in history. Once the doors to the past opened, dreams became a processing point to let go of the accumulation of thousands of years of lifetimes that were longing for release.

To try this on your own, start with the *hoku* point—the area at the base of your thumb and first finger. Hold this point and at the same time, close your eyes and relax. Allow colors, images, memories, and emotions to bubble up. If you don't get any response from that point, continue on your own to different points in your body. You don't have to be a shiatsu practitioner or an acupuncturist. Simply put pressure on various parts of your body until you find a place where your thumb (or fingers) seems to sink in, and then repeat the exercise.

Past Lives and Weight Loss

I was so excited about my clients' results that I began to use past-life regressions in my personal life. At the time, I had a weight problem and was constantly dieting. I could lose about ten pounds, but I'd inevitably gain them back. When I discovered the power of regression, I took myself back to a specific time in my childhood. There I saw myself at the age of three being told by my mother what a "big girl" I was. This was her way of letting me know that I met with her approval. Thus, I subconsciously equated "big" with "good."

As an adult, I naturally wanted to be good, so I was subconsciously helping my body remain big. Once I'd made that realization, I lost 15 pounds without even trying! But I still didn't weigh what I felt was ideal for me. I kept struggling to meet my goal but didn't have success. At that point, I had another startling revelation in a dream. My dream was very vivid:

Dust assailed my nostrils. Billows of golden dust surrounded a buffalo herd as it stampeded by. I felt rooted to the land, and strangely, the buffalo charge seemed to reflect the restless stirring in my soul.

Waking up from this dramatic dream, I felt that in my night hours I'd been transported over the bridge of time to a past life as a Native American woman. The images and smells were so real; the shimmering colors around me seemed alive. In my waking hours, I used that dream as a starting point to regress to an earlier life where I discovered that I was a member of a wandering Blackfoot tribe. I saw myself as an old woman with a serious hip problem, and as a consequence, I walked with a limp. After having the dream, I began to see how many of the habits in my current life could be traced back to my Blackfoot life.

We were a nomadic tribe, constantly moving to find food. In the winter, there wasn't always enough. Even when there was enough, there was an eating hierarchy. The male elders ate first, then the chiefs and warriors, and finally the younger women and children. As an old and physically impaired woman, I was often the last to eat and would go to sleep hungry.

I saw how this past-life experience set in motion a present-day pattern. During mealtimes in my current life, whenever there was a communal dish rather than individual servings, I felt intense panic. I was afraid that I wouldn't get enough to eat, and when I was served, I'd eat voraciously—even if I wasn't hungry. This created physical problems: Since I ate so fast, the food wasn't digested properly, and I was also eating more than my body needed. In those moments of panic, I was reenacting my memories of not having enough to eat. However, experiencing my relationship with food in my life as a Blackfoot Indian helped me understand my present relationship with food. As I released the belief that I wasn't going to get enough, I was able to slow down and start eating more in accordance with my body's needs rather than out of an old fear about survival.

In my life as an old Indian woman, my hip problem soon prevented me from keeping up with the tribe during their moves from camp to camp. It was a tribal tradition to leave frail people when they could no longer keep up, so I was eventually left behind to die.

Consciously, as a Native American woman, I understood this. I knew that it was necessary to leave the old behind to ensure the survival of the rest of the tribe. However, in that life, I subconsciously experienced anguish, loneliness, and the bitterness of betrayal. These feelings were at odds with my acceptance of the ways of the tribe, so I suppressed them.

The images and feelings from my life as a Blackfoot were very clear. I starved and froze to death with feelings of extreme resentment and loneliness. The emotions and choices that we have at death are powerful and often carry forward through many lifetimes. However, it's not *all* of our emotions that are carried forward. It's the suppressed ones—those we didn't allow ourselves to experience and express at the time—that create present-day blockages.

It wasn't my starving to death that created my weight problem—it was the suppressed emotions that I'd carried into my current life. Recalling that Blackfoot memory, I was able to understand why, every time I'd tried to diet in this life, I felt incredibly lonely. Subconsciously, I equated a lack of food with being abandoned and alone. When I finally allowed myself to experience those painful, suppressed feelings from that former life, I lost the remaining pounds I'd wanted to lose!

Furthermore, I've found that past-life regression is an excellent adjunct to any weight-loss program for those interested in keeping the pounds off. Some 95 percent of people who lose weight through dieting gain it back again. But those who lose weight by going to the emotional source of the problem—which is often in a past life—are usually able to keep it off much longer, if not forever.

Twenty-five years later, after I went through menopause, the pounds packed on again. It happened so gradually that I wasn't aware of it. When I finally took stock and realized that something had to be done, I once again journeyed into my past lives to discover a lifetime in India where, as an ascetic, I was very thin . . . and extremely hungry. I swore over and over in that life that in my future life I'd be spiritual, but *without ever having to be hungry.* I guess I got my wish! I'm still overweight, and still fulfilling that impassioned, starving ascetic's vow. And I've come to a comfortable acceptance and love of my body just as it is.

How Uncovering My Past Life
Healed My Current Life

Discovering my past life as a Blackfoot enabled me to remove other barriers in my present life. Whenever the tribe moved, we were required to carry heavy things over long distances. In my present life, I was always carrying heavy things, often when I didn't need to. Sometimes I'd even pick up a large stone and carry it for a distance, for no apparent reason. Not only was this a peculiar habit, but it was damaging my spine, too. As soon as I recognized where this pattern came from, I no longer felt a compulsion to carry heavy items.

In my life as a Blackfoot woman, I was a healer, administering herbs, attending births, and soothing wounds (all things that I've done in this life). Although I was an excellent healer, my hip problem made me feel unworthy of marriage, as I seemed to equate physical ability with worthiness. I never married in that life, and I blamed the tribe for that, thinking it was they who saw me as unworthy.

However, when I was transported into that life as a Blackfoot, I realized that it was not the tribe's judgment but my own that had made me turn suitors away. *I* had felt unworthy of love. In my present life, from early childhood I'd assumed that I'd never marry. Later, my injuries from the shooting made me feel undesirable as a woman, further promoting my belief that I'd never marry. Traveling back in time to that point where I made the initial decision, and then reliving it, seemed to magically lift my lifelong blockage to having a long and fulfilling relationship. I now have a wonderful husband, the man of my dreams, to whom I've been married for 34 years.

In my present life, so many things shifted once the door to that Blackfoot life swung open. I'd always suffered from poor circulation in my feet and hands, even in warm climates like that of Hawaii. This was a legacy from my freezing to death in that earlier life. I also found that whenever I got cold, I felt isolated and emotionally numb. I never could understand winter sports such as skiing—it didn't make sense to me that people would *choose* to be cold.

After changing the decisions I'd made in that past life, my circulation improved so much that it's now much better than most people's. And I love winter sports. In fact, cross-country skiing is probably about as close as I come to connecting with the Creator. I love the pure white blanket of snow and the stillness of a snow-shrouded forest. It's wonderful to watch the soft crystals float from a high branch when a gentle breeze shakes the tree. I would have missed all this joy had I not explored that past life.

Another old pattern that began to dissolve, after seeing my Blackfoot life, was my strong need to be included in group activities and to get everyone to like me—even if it meant denying what I knew intuitively to be right.

I was voted *nicest girl* in high school, which at that time seemed like an immense honor. Later, however, I recognized what it really meant. In my subconscious was a core belief that if people liked me, I'd survive. So to get everyone to accept me, I gave up much of my own truth. When I was dying as an old Native American woman, I kept thinking that if my fellow tribe members had liked me more, perhaps I wouldn't have been left behind. So I came into this life believing that I *must* have everyone's acceptance. Eventually, I realized that I didn't have to attain everyone's approval to find my truth, which allowed for an enormous transformation in my life.

Each past life contains seeds that sprout in our current lives. Dying cold and hungry—and feeling betrayed—in my life as a Blackfoot created an emotional charge regarding betrayal. In my younger years in my current life, I manifested situation after situation in which I felt spurned. And in each of these episodes, I became a whirlpool of emotions, overcome with rage, bitterness, resentment, sadness, and grief. In every situation in which I felt jilted, I later found that *I actually hadn't been betrayed.*

This was the same pattern that occurred in my life as a Blackfoot Indian. I wasn't betrayed; I knew that if I couldn't keep up, I'd be left. I knew that this was a tribal law to which I adhered. I wasn't actually betrayed, but I felt that I was.

We keep re-creating the same patterns through our various lifetimes until we release them from our personal energy fields. I no longer create situations in which I feel betrayed. But if I did, I believe that I'd now be an observer, watching an old pattern unfold rather than being engulfed in the negative emotions that used to surround those situations.

After my exploration into my past life as a Native American woman, I began to understand my interest in herbs. I used to own an herb company and still use herbs for healing. I also understood my deep love of nature. I realized why I collected antlers. Native Americans used antlers for many things, including tools—subconsciously, I still feel the value of these beautiful creations.

I now understand my love for drums and drum rituals. I can trace so many of my present views back to my existence as a Blackfoot. In my life, I've led ceremonial sessions such as medicine-wheel ceremonies, vision quests, and sweat lodges, as well as teaching drumming, drum making, and drum painting. All of this gave me great joy. In my present life, I've pulled forth what was beautiful and sacred from that past life and incorporated it into my current circumstances. Not only is it valuable to release limiting patterns from the past, but you can also activate talents and abilities from those times.

In my life now, I have Cherokee blood running through me, and in my earlier life, I was also a Native American. In my past-life regressions with patients, I've found that our present-day roots can often give clues about former lives. In the past, being a Native American entailed hard times and difficulty, but in my life now, I'm proud of being Cherokee, and this ancestry only brings me joy. Honoring my heritage now has helped heal the difficulty that I had in the past.

Vows of Poverty in a Past Life
Affect Your Present Life

Later, I experienced another past life that was dramatically influencing my finances in my present one. For most of my younger adult life, I'd struggled with finances and possessions. As soon as I received any money or was given any material object, I seemed to find a reason for giving it away. I had an incessant need to be without possessions and money. Another aspect of this was my choice of clothing: I wore the same style of clothes day in and day out and was reluctant to buy anything new.

When I was visiting Italy in the 1970s, I had an incredible déjà vu experience that convinced me that I'd been a Franciscan monk on a small island off Venice. Seeing that life, I understood why I had difficulty creating abundance in this one.

I was in Italy for a conference but had a few days of downtime, so a friend and I hired a gondolier who ferried us around to the various islands just off the coast of Venice. One particular place that we stopped at was St. Francis Island, which is entirely a Franciscan monastery. The instant my feet touched the ground, I absolutely knew that I'd been there before and was overwhelmed with images of a life there. It was so clear and real. The head monk, who spoke English, validated my vision. As he showed me around, I spontaneously expressed surprise about one of the "new" buildings. He looked at me in astonishment that I'd know this . . . and explained that it was new to the original structure, but it was more than 600 years old.

As I walked on the beautiful monastery grounds during my visit, I instinctively remembered many details about my life as a monk. It was as if I were transported back through time.

My life was simple yet filled with a deep, rich peace. I lived in a small cell, and I loved working in the garden. I had strong feelings about morality. Money and possessions were wrong; poverty was good. Poor people were God's chosen ones.

Anything that you strongly judge as right or wrong will attach itself to you lifetime after lifetime. In that past life, I'd taken vows of poverty and decided that owning material objects was immoral. *Any vow that you take in your past lives will continue to influence you in a powerful way until you release the hold it has on you.*

The vow of poverty I'd taken when I was a monk continued to rule my life. In my present life, whenever I was given a gift, I felt uncomfortable and anxious and had a compulsion to give it away. My subconscious memories of the vows were influencing my current existence to the point where I couldn't allow myself to own anything of value.

The energy from that past life proved to be a very strong influence in this one. In addition to the two years I'd lived in a Zen monastery in my early 20s, I spent long periods of time in solitude and retreat. Even when I wasn't living in a monastery, I dressed in clothes similar to that of the Franciscan monks. Every day I put on a long brown tunic made of rough woven cotton over brown pants of the same material, and I also had large rustic sandals. I wore this outfit to work, at home, and even to weddings and other special events. When I did a self-regression and released the vows that I made in that past life, I acquired the freedom to create abundance in my current life.

Material things in themselves aren't bad—it's our attachment to or identification with them that causes difficulty. After releasing my vows of poverty, I felt the liberty to choose what I wanted—and didn't want—to have in my life. I was no longer being controlled by a past decision. I could decide whether or not I wanted to have possessions . . . and could do so without feeling guilty. The vows that you make in former lives have an enormous effect on you. It's valuable to recognize and release any limiting vows from past lives that may still have a hold on you.

Group Regression—Meeting Others You've Known Before

I was so encouraged by my clients' results and those in my own life that I accepted an offer to teach a course about past lives. I began to do group regressions in these classes and was amazed to see that the same, if not better, effects were produced with large groups of people. I worked with between 100 and 1,000 people at a time—usually averaging around 200. I began to notice that over and over again in these groups, many people who sat next to each other would often experience past lives in the same country and period in history. It was as if they had subconsciously decided to come together once again at this exciting juncture to release not only individual karma, but also collective karma.

This idea is based on the theory that you incarnate lifetime after lifetime with the same individuals. These souls can be likened to a flock of birds that migrates to distant countries yet always flies together. Information gathered in my reincarnation seminars has consistently shown that individuals incarnate in groups and tend to be drawn together lifetime after lifetime.

A striking example of this occurred in Canberra, Australia, a number of years ago. I was conducting a past-life seminar that included a regression meditation. During these types of meditations, I don't give any clues that might predispose someone toward a particular past life or time in history. For example, I might say something nonspecific during the meditation such as, "You're standing in the mists of time, and when the mists lift, you'll be in one of your past lives." After a process of this sort, I take a show of hands to see what the seminar participants had experienced.

Astoundingly, in that seminar in Canberra, more than two-thirds of the 100 people in the room felt that during the regression they'd experienced a past life in Rome! I hadn't mentioned Rome before the process. On examination, it seemed plausible that individuals who in a past life had lived in ancient Rome (a planned city that was a center of government, peopled by many government employees) would have chosen to incarnate in Canberra (also a planned city that's a center of government, peopled by many government employees).

At a past-life seminar in Seattle, an inordinate number of people said that they'd been World War II fighter pilots. At another seminar, a larger number said that they'd been American Pilgrims, and at yet another, an astounding majority of people had all been Chinese field-workers. I don't feel that these are coincidences; in fact, I believe that long before this current life, the participants at each seminar made a choice to come together again, as a group, in order to release limitations from shared past lives.

I received a letter recently from a woman in Germany who had a noteworthy experience while attending a past-life workshop that I'd presented in Australia. During my seminars, I play music and then ask the participants to walk around the room. I tell them that when the music stops, they may very well be standing next to someone they knew in a past life. Most people think this is ridiculous, but they do the exercise anyway. Ursula wrote to say that when the music stopped, she was *coincidentally* standing next to another German. There were more than 200 people in the seminar, and she hadn't seen this man before.

As they talked, they realized that they'd been born in the same small village! While she was growing up, she'd walked past his house every day on her way to school. In addition, they had each moved to Canada to the same town at approximately the same time—and they had each moved to the same town in Australia at the same time. Now this could be an amazing coincidence, or it could lend credence to the idea that we're attracted to the same souls lifetime after lifetime. Ursula's letter isn't unusual—I've received hundreds of similar ones from people who've attended my reincarnation workshops.

Sometimes at the end of a session, I'll ask if there's anyone who wants to describe what they saw during their past-life meditation. At a London seminar, a man said that he'd seen himself as a Native American standing on a cliff. Then another Native American crept up and pushed him over the edge. As he said this, the man sitting next to him (whom he didn't know) went very pale.

I asked this man, "What did *you* experience during the past-life process?"

He answered in a quavering voice, "I was an American Indian, and *I* was pushing someone off a cliff!"

On another occasion, a woman said that she remembered a life in 19th-century London in which she was in a public park pushing someone in an old wooden wheelchair. The woman next to her looked startled and said that she recalled a life during the same time period in London, and she was in a public park being *pushed* in an old wooden wheelchair! One man relived an experience as a native of the Amazon jungle. He recalled helping his tribe destroy an entire neighboring village. The person seated beside him (a stranger) had experienced watching his Amazon village being wiped out by a neighboring tribe.

I found that in large groups, tremendous energy can be generated that makes it easier for past-life exploration and personal healing. Whenever possible, I work with the energy of the room using ancient clearing techniques. (For more information about this, please see my books *Sacred Space, Space Clearing A–Z,* and *Feng Shui for the Soul.*) I also like to place healers around the room during regressions to help generate healing energy and love so that people's experiences are positive, empowering, and promote well-being. I'm now teaching traditional therapists how to incorporate past-life regression techniques into their work. The growing interest in reincarnation by the Western world gives credence to the idea that as we face the future, there's a collective need to understand where we've come from so we're better prepared for what lies ahead.

There's immense value to be gained in going to a past-life coach or attending a past-life seminar; however, you can begin your exploration right now in your own home by using the simple exercises that are described in this book. Many people have reported dynamic positive changes in life by following these simple techniques.

Just reading this book, even *without* doing the exercises, can also contribute to the healing of unresolved issues. This occurs because as you focus on understanding your earlier lives, subconsciously you activate old past-life patterns. This reenactment of past-life situations (which may appear in your dreams or in the outer circumstance of your life) is both healing and strengthening. There's never been a more powerful time in the evolution of our planet to resolve old issues and negative programming. By focusing on your former lives—and using the methods described in this book—you can heal the past and thus embrace your future with joy . . . and be open for the miracles that will flow into your life.

Chapter Two

REINCARNATION AND KARMA

The concept of reincarnation, which is the center of past-life therapy, has been with us since before recorded history. It's the doctrine or belief that an essential part—the higher self, or the soul—of each human being survives death and is reborn in another body. Although a new identity develops in each life, there's a spiritual part of the being that remains constant throughout successive lives.

Current estimates suggest that at least a third of the people alive today believe that the soul is eternal and repeatedly returns to Earth through rebirth into new bodies in order to grow and learn. A recent Harris Poll of the spiritual beliefs of Americans found that 27 percent believe in reincarnation—that is, they believe they were once another person. This includes 40 percent of people aged 25 to 29 but only 14 percent of individuals aged 65 and over (which indicates that the belief in reincarnation is growing among our youth).

The spiritual belief in an enduring "self" that incarnates again and again declares that each lifetime provides a wealth of experiences that allow us as divine beings to become stronger, more balanced, and more loving. And eventually, we reunite with Spirit. (At times I prefer to use the words *Spirit* or *Creator* instead of *God* because some people equate God with a male deity in the sky who's judgmental. To me, the words *God, Goddess, the Creator, Great Spirit, Spirit,* and *Cosmic Consciousness* all mean the same thing—which is the living force within all things.)

Spontaneous reincarnation episodes can occur in many ways. Have you ever had the eerie experience of being in a strange town and feeling a recognition almost too deep to describe? Have you ever heard a particular piece of music and felt transported by it or had a vivid dream about a time in history or a foreign country that seemed extraordinarily familiar and real? All these incidents could have their roots in past lifetimes.

In one life, perhaps you were very poor and thus had a chance to learn humility and resourcefulness firsthand. In another, you might have been wealthy in order to understand how to deal with money fairly and positively. You may have been blind in order to activate your inner sight, or athletic to experience and comprehend physical strength. You might have been a woman in one life and a man in another—or Caucasian in one and

Asian in another. Try to think of past lives not so much as building blocks but as pieces of a jigsaw puzzle, with each piece a lifetime making you more balanced.

Reincarnation and History

Throughout history, great thinkers have pondered the mysteries of life, birth, and rebirth. The earliest record of the theory of reincarnation, which comes from ancient Egypt, says that the soul is immortal; when the body perishes, the soul enters into another human body. Both early and present-day Hindus believe that the soul is immortal and inhabits one body after another in search of its true divine nature. Centuries before Christ, Buddha taught about the cycle of reincarnation—the great wheel of life and death. Like Hindus and Sikhs, Buddhists strive to be released from the death/rebirth cycle by attaining nirvana, or oneness with the Creator. In addition, the Essenes, an early Jewish sect; the medieval Christian Cathari, who flourished in France; and Islamic Sufis are also said to have embraced the idea of reincarnation.

The Greek philosopher Pythagoras, who lived some five centuries before Christ, not only wrote about this subject but also described his personal recollections of his various incarnations. His fellow philosopher Plato was also a believer. Napoléon claimed to have been the 8th-century Holy Roman emperor Charlemagne in a past life. The French philosopher Voltaire observed that "it's not more surprising to be born twice than once." The Spanish surrealist painter Salvador Dalí said that he believed he'd been the great Spanish mystic St. John of the Cross. And the 18th-century German writer and poet

Johann Wolfgang von Goethe deeply embraced the idea of past lives as well: "I am certain that I've been here, as I am now, a thousand times before, and I hope to return a thousand times." Many famous Americans, including Benjamin Franklin and Thomas Edison, also gave credence to reincarnation.

George S. Patton, the famous American World War II general, believed that he'd been the Carthaginian general Hannibal in a previous life. Henry Ford, the father of modern assembly lines and mass production, was convinced that he'd lived before, too; and his most recent life had been as a soldier killed during the Battle of Gettysburg. Ralph Waldo Emerson, the American poet and essayist, subscribed to the notion of reincarnation.

Reincarnation as a viable personal belief system is becoming more prevalent in Western culture, as many people find that their spiritual needs aren't being met by current religions. Disillusioned individuals are turning instead to this philosophy, which answers questions such as "Why do we keep repeating the same negative patterns? Where do our recurring fears and phobias come from? Why do we feel an instant attraction to some people and places?" And more important, it helps to answer the question "What is our purpose here on Earth?" The concept of reincarnation allows us to understand the way in which we each weave our own destiny.

Soul Mates

One of the most important aspects of life that this philosophy addresses is that of relationships. Understanding and healing emotional difficulties—which have their roots in past lives—can help improve the quality of our present relationships. Our current partners, who are our karmic counterparts, give us the chance to complete unfinished tasks and help us release negative thoughts and emotions that intrude into this lifetime. Those with whom we have relationships that originated in a past life are called our "soul mates."

Have you ever had a brief encounter that left such an intense impression that you could never quite shake off the memory? Many years ago as I was standing in line to see a film, a tall man emerged from the darkness and walked past me. I didn't even see his face. My breath stopped short, my knees went weak, and I felt like I was about to faint. When I turned to look at him, he was gone. Who was this man who inspired such an extraordinary response in me? A psychologist might say that I had activated a hidden memory from childhood of someone who resembled that tall stranger—however, it's also likely that he was a soul mate.

How many times have you caught a brief glimpse of someone across a crowded room and felt an instant rapport—an inner knowing that you've encountered a kindred spirit? In that brief moment, did you feel a yearning to rekindle those memories from the past and hold on to them for eternity? On the other hand, have you ever met someone and instantly felt uncomfortable, confused, or perhaps even angry for no apparent reason?

Such meetings are part of a complex web of intrigue that lies deep within our subconscious minds and dictates the tapestries of events that weave their way throughout our lifetimes. Our past-life relationships determine how we interact with those around us. They may also cause us to feel intense love or desire for an individual—or hatred, envy, or spite for another. As the soul memories are roused, relationships are rekindled. And almost everyone we connect with in this life is likely to have been involved in many of our past lives—perhaps as a brother, sister, parent, colleague, child, lover, or even an enemy.

The dynamics of our former-life situations are recreated in our present lives; and they may be passionate, romantic, and adventurous or even angry and vengeful. When we meet familiar souls in this current lifetime, it's to relive and rework the relationship. Those familiar eyes across a crowded room are often an inner reminder of the individuals whom we've chosen to interact with once more, and the encounter provides us with the opportunity to reexperience those karmic bonds.

The idea of a soul mate usually evokes images of Romeo and Juliet, Tristan and Isolde, or Katharine Hepburn and Spencer Tracy—individuals who found their perfect complement, becoming symbols of exquisite love that seem to transcend time and space. Although the term *soul mate* is commonly used to describe the one great love of your life, I believe that soul mates are actually *all* the individuals you've been with in past lives and even in other dimensions. This idea is based on the theory that you incarnate with the same individuals. You and your soul mates enter a lifetime together and are attracted to each other even from the far reaches of the world.

My first understanding of how soul mates are drawn to one another occurred when I was a young college student in the Midwest. I was very much in love with a man who taught sociology at the university. We lived together and shared a small country home, but eventually I sensed that he was seeing another woman. I was so distraught that I decided to relocate to Hawaii in order to put the soured love affair behind me.

I later moved to a different address in Hawaii and then one day, over tea with a friendly neighbor, I discovered that my new acquaintance and I had gone to the same university. We even knew some of the same people. As she began talking about a clandestine affair she'd had with a teacher in the sociology department, the truth slowly dawned on me—she was the woman my lover had had an affair with. Fortunately, the situation was far enough behind us so that we could still become good friends. These kinds of stories aren't uncommon—on the contrary, people who've been together before somehow find each other in the most unusual circumstances.

There's a tendency to think that our destined partners are the only ones whom we feel an instant attraction to; however, in my regression work, I've found that soul mates can also be the people we experience difficulties with in our present lives. In fact, such challenging individuals are often the ones we've had the most intimate past-life connections with.

When soul mates meet, there's usually instant rapport, recognition, or even repulsion. If there was a sexual liaison in a past life, there will likely be a physical attraction in the present life—sometimes an almost explosive and intense one. Although soul mates don't always see eye to eye, there's usually a sense of familiarity in the relationship. They'll often have a communication beyond logical explanation and a deep attachment (either negative or positive) that is sometimes telepathic.

Love Mates

One of the greatest mysteries in the philosophy of reincarnation is the idea that every human being has a perfect partner. This person has been called a *love mate, dual mate, twin flame,* and most often, a *soul mate.* Researchers have stated that even in religions dating back to the Stone Age, one of the main reasons for leading a positive life was so that one could be reborn near his or her true love in the next life. The writer and poet Goethe also wrote a book based on the medieval idea that couples were divinely united. *Die Wahlverwandtschaften,* which is usually translated as *Elective Affinities,* contends that every individual has a perfect mate waiting to be discovered.

A commonly held theory regarding love mates is that we were originally androgynous beings—souls that were neither male nor female. Somewhere in time we were split in two and became either male or female energy but not necessarily two distinct bodies. These halves set forth into the Earth plane—a division of polarities growing and expanding, forever striving to reunite. The constant drive toward procreation is seen as a deep spiritual urge for that primal union and for the experience of oneness that occurred before the separation.

Those who adhere to this theory contend that there will be an increase in the search for and reunion with love mates in the coming years due to the increase in the vibratory rate of the planet. This accounts for the rise in relationships that transcend differences in race, age, gender, religion, and social standing.

Sometimes a love mate can be in the spirit world rather than in a physical body, offering assistance from the "other side." This can account for the feeling that a loving presence is watching over you. Soul mates can also be the same sex, although one will usually have the negative (feminine) polarity, while the other has the positive (masculine) polarity.

In spite of the allure of so-called perfect love, it's a mistake to spend your life waiting for your "true" love. First of all, this attitude keeps you from experiencing the joy in the moment because you're living in a kind of *waiting mode.* (Incidentally, when you're in that stalled mode, it's almost impossible for love to find you in the here-and-now because you're so focused on the future.)

Second, love mates usually don't have smooth-sailing relationships; in fact, they can be quite stormy because our partners act as mirrors, emphasizing or reflecting back to us those aspects of ourselves that we dislike. For this reason, when love mates come together, the relationship isn't always enduring. However, when they truly unite, for whatever length of time, there's a matching of the heart and soul that is fathomless.

The degree to which you accept and love yourself plays an important role in your success in finding your love mate. If you feel unworthy while attempting to attract your destined partner, you'll start to think, *There must be something wrong with this person if he (or she) loves me.* You'll then subconsciously begin to find things wrong with the other person and push him or her away. Your love mate could even be the person you've been married to for the past 20 years, but you haven't been able to see the truth.

For many people, the philosophy of reincarnation and soul mates provides an understanding of why we're here. It can give us insight into our current relationships and offer answers to some of life's seemingly unanswerable questions.

The Law of Karma

Intrinsic to the understanding of reincarnation is the comprehension of the concept "As ye sow, so shall ye reap." This is the principle that governs karma. It's the fate we create for ourselves as a result of our judgments and actions in this life and in previous ones. Karma is the law of cause and effect—the universal ruling system that determines how we weave our destiny. It allows us to understand why one person is constantly dealt adversity, while another has a seemingly easy path.

In the past, karma was viewed as a kind of cosmic accounting system of debits and credits—a punitive and retributive law. Many once believed that all suffering was the result of previous wrongdoing—anything negative in one's life was caused by karma. Those of us who were handicapped, had incurable diseases, or endured endless suffering were all thought to be paying back for some terrible harm that we perpetrated in a past life. However, this belief does a terrible injustice to anyone in an unfortunate situation.

The idea that karma is God's punitive system is now changing. The current opinion is much more compassionate and humane. There isn't an authority in the sky who decides what's right and wrong for each individual. Instead, inside each of us is an inner scale of justice monitoring our integrity. We're our own judge and jury, always trying to balance the scales—there isn't a stern deity presiding over us. Our inner wisdom deems whether our actions are appropriate. The verdict isn't always what we *consciously* assume is right at the time, even if it's condoned by our religious or cultural beliefs. There are much deeper inner truths we adhere to, and sometimes they're beyond the rules of society.

I believe that we create not only our reality, but also our karma. For example, if you cheated someone in a past life and haven't made peace with this act, then you may feel unworthy and deserving of punishment. So in your present life, you may subconsciously create difficult situations and find yourself being taken advantage of. I don't believe that this is cosmic punishment—it's a kind of inner balancing. When you feel deceived, you then have the opportunity to develop compassion for others who have had a similar experience. The extent to which you can accept yourself and all of your actions—and take responsibility for them (no matter what lifetime they occurred in)—is the extent to which you can step beyond karma. In other words, you've fulfilled your karma when you unconditionally forgive and accept yourself and others.

Forgiveness is the key to stepping off the karmic treadmill. (Remember, you don't need to forgive the act—because some are unforgivable—but it's important to forgive the individual or people who committed it.)

The Native American View of Karma

The ancient Native American view of karma is slightly different from the Western and Eastern views. In this tradition, one's actions in life were made with the understanding of how they might affect the entire tribe and the following seven generations. As I mentioned earlier, *what you sow is what you reap.* For example, if early Native Americans wanted to cut down a tree, they'd first think about how that would impact their descendants. In some tribes, inappropriate acts weren't physically punished; instead, the offender would take part in numerous discussions with tribal elders until the full consequences of his or her behavior were understood.

Native Americans believed that each and every action affected the whole of life. They intuitively understood that everything is connected, we live in a viable universe, and all life is interrelated. The flutter of a butterfly's wings in the Rocky Mountains can affect the tornadoes of the Philippines, which can affect a nursing baby in a small village in Italy.

Those ancient native people understood that every act had consequences. This idea applies to the physical world as well as to the ways of man. Newton's third law of motion exhibits this, stating that every action has a reaction, which is equal and opposite. In the realm of karma, the power of our thoughts and feelings is palpable and has a life of its own—it has form and substance in the causal world. Depending on the intensity, passion, and clarity of the mind of the thinker, every thought creates ripples in the energy field of the planet. In other words, it's not just what you *do*, it's also what you *think* and *feel*. Actions, thoughts, and words generate waves of energy that echo throughout the universe. In this way, we're constantly creating and balancing karma.

Manifestations of Karma

Karma can manifest itself in different ways. It can be demonstrated symbolically: People who in a past life were never willing to see the truth about themselves and the world around them might be born physically blind in a new life in order to learn how to perceive truth through intuition and feeling. A Viking warrior from centuries ago might have cruelly shed the blood of others in battle, but in a future life he may develop anemia. I had a young client who couldn't swallow easily; through regression, we discovered that in a past life as a dancer she was forced into a situation that she couldn't swallow *emotionally*.

Karma can be a means of balancing the scales, too. For example, a woman who had been a lady-in-waiting during the Renaissance always sped through relationships in that life without taking the time to listen to others. But in this life, she feels that no one ever listens to her.

Some afflictions and difficulties don't necessarily come into the *symbolic* or *scale-balancing* categories. For instance, an individual with a physical affliction might incarnate in order to be of service to others. A child born with Down syndrome may be an evolved being who has incarnated to allow people to experience the gift of giving.

I'm sometimes asked about karma associated with the most devastating event—the death of a child. I can't image anything more painful, and I'm always grieved when I hear of it. I believe that there are two reasons why a child might die young. The first is that the little one came here as a service to his or her family and friends. When a child passes, everyone touched by the death usually undergoes an enormous amount of soul-

47

searching and has a profound shift of consciousness. Although devastating, this process usually promotes spiritual growth. The second reason is that the child who dies is an evolved soul who doesn't need a long lifetime. He or she just requires a short period of physical existence to round off the Earth-plane experience. I believe that a soul contract is made with the parents and other family members before the spirit incarnates. Although much pain ensues, powerful spiritual growth arises from this extremely difficult event.

Instant Karma

Be aware before passing judgment, for often the very thing that you criticize will become a part of your life until you accept and forgive the foibles of others. I'll give you a simple example: In a grocery store one day I heard a mother shouting angrily at her young child. I found that extremely upsetting and thought she was wrong to do it. I might have even given her a look that said, *What you're doing is bad!*

Several weeks later I was out shopping when my young daughter started driving me to distraction, and *I* began yelling at her—then suddenly I stopped. In that moment, I was filled with deep compassion for that other mother I had quickly judged. The world is an infinitely better place when we don't criticize the actions of others, but instead imagine walking in their shoes. Native Americans say: "Walk a mile in my moccasins."

As life on our planet continues to speed up, we'll find ourselves balancing the karmic scales faster. I call this "instant karma." For example, if you judge someone for being inarticulate, the *next day* you may find yourself in a situation where your words seem jumbled and unclear. It's not a punishment, but rather your way of creating a circumstance that will allow you to be more understanding and less critical of others. And this phenomenon will happen faster and faster in the years ahead, as there is an increasing momentum toward completion. You'll find instant karma occurring more often in your life! It's a way of measuring your rate of spiritual growth—and the higher you rate, the quicker your thoughts will manifest and your judgments will return to you. Incomplete relationships and unfinished business, both in this life and in past lives, will move to the forefront for long-awaited resolution.

Going Through More Than One Lifetime in the Same Body

I believe that because of this quickening pace, many people are going through more than one lifetime within this evolutionary cycle. They have so much karma they want to complete that many are going through several lifetimes during their present life.

For example, in the past a man might have been born in a certain village, taken on the same occupation as his father and grandfather, gotten married, and eventually died—all in the same village. Now someone might spend half of his or her life making a living as a cook in Brazil and the second half working as a psychologist in Greece. Each half of the life could have an entirely different agenda and could fulfill completely different karmic situations.

In any discussion of karma, it's important to bring up a viewpoint that many people hold: *I can't do anything about it. It's my karma.* No matter how difficult your life is, no matter what hardships you've endured, *you're not stuck with your situation.* You have the free will to change your circumstances or the way in which you view them. You're not bound to unalterable situations—the past, present, and future are malleable. You *can* change your karma and your resulting life circumstances.

Destiny and Free Will

I believe that each of us is born with a predestined future, and on the day we're born our date of death has already been decreed. My father's mother was an astrologer who had trained with a remarkable man named Manly Hall. My grandmother said that she had seen her own death in her astrological chart, and I don't think she was surprised when her time came to leave her body.

However, as fervently as I believe in predestination, I also believe in free will. And I don't have difficulty holding these two seemingly divergent perspectives. In fact, I believe that the more opposing points of view you can be open to, the more compassionate a human being you are. Beyond linear time there's a changeable future *and* past, and it's possible to shift consciousness so that you can choose an entirely different timeline with a new subsequent past and future. In other words, you're not stuck with your past, and your future can be altered. (This is discussed more thoroughly in Chapter 10: "Future Lives, the Ripple Effect, and Miracles.")

In the book *Autobiography of a Yogi,* Paramahansa Yogananda writes about astrology and karma. He states that one's astrological chart can show all the past karma that one has accrued, lifetime after lifetime. He writes: "A child is born on that day and at that hour when the celestial rays are in mathematical harmony with his individual karma." He also states that through prayer, spiritual practice, and correct conduct, you can convert difficult karma, so what might have yielded the thrust of a sword can become the thrust of a pin. However, Yogananda warns that those astrologers who can accurately decipher your karma from your astrological chart *are few.*

I've had some amazing experiences that make a solid case for predestination. When I was in southern Africa conducting seminars and meeting members of the Zulu tribe, I met a very special Dutch woman who talked about having spent time in India. During her visits there, she heard of a remarkable place in the distant mountains where, generations ago, a famous astrologer once lived, and where his descendants had kept his records intact for hundreds of years. When the writing would become faded, they'd meticulously recopy the papers.

During this astrologer's life, whenever someone consulted him for a reading, not only did he compose a current chart, but he also drew up charts for their *future* lifetimes! So if you were lucky enough to have been one of his original clients hundreds of years ago, you could have read the chart for one of your future lives—although it wouldn't occur for many generations. He told his clients that if they came to retrieve their records in their future lives, they would be available for them.

At first I thought that this sounded almost too amazing to be true. Perhaps the legend was a ruse to make money so members of the poor village could earn a living. When I voiced these concerns, however, the Dutch woman told me that not only was no one ever charged for the charts, but visitors weren't even allowed to present flowers or other gifts.

She explained to me that she'd decided to travel to the astrologer's village with a friend. When she arrived, she told the villagers her place of birth and her birth date. They searched but weren't able to locate her chart— therefore, they concluded that she wasn't one of the individuals who'd had their charts prepared hundreds of years earlier. They did, however, find her friend's chart.

In her friend's present life, he had a very painful skin condition; and in his chart it said that during his incarnation in the 20th century, he would have a skin disease because he hadn't been kind to lepers in a previous life. According to the chart, he must give generously to patients with leprosy in order to get rid of it. When he returned home from India, he donated to causes that were connected to this disease, and his skin condition completely cleared up. But when he eventually stopped giving to those charities, his skin problem returned.

I would have regarded this as no more than an interesting story, except that only a month later I heard a similar tale. I was in London giving a series of lectures on reincarnation when I was asked to take part in a BBC radio program with Eve Pollard, the editor of the *Sunday Mirror* and *Sunday Express,* in which individuals from different backgrounds participated in lively discussions on various topics. One of the other guests was a man who originally came from India. At the end of the show, this soft-spoken Indian gentleman, who was a doctor and very famous sculptor, said, "There's something that I'd like to show you."

As we sat in the studio lobby, he pulled out a sheaf of faded papers torn at the edges. The pages were covered in script that I assumed was ancient Sanskrit. The doctor then proceeded to tell me that when he was 19 years old, he'd traveled with his father to a place where astrological records had been kept for hundreds of years. It sounded like the same place that the Dutch woman had described to me. After a long and arduous journey, the doctor and his father arrived on a rainy day, which was an unusual occurrence in that part of the world. They located the astrological charts for their present lives and found that both had indeed been clients of the famous astrologer hundreds of years before. The doctor told me that his chart stated that he'd come to claim his records *when he was 19 years old, on a rainy day.* His chart also correctly gave his name in his present life.

As we looked over his well-worn chart, I said, "You've had this chart for some 30 years? Has it been accurate?"

He went carefully through the chart with me (although I only had his word for what it said, as I can't read Sanskrit) and showed me many examples of where it had been accurate. I pass these stories along to you as they were shared with me. I found both individuals to be honest, trustworthy people. I believe them and their accounts.

Transmigration: Can Someone Have a Past Life as an Animal?

I'm often asked if we've always been human beings in past lives, and I've found that it's not unusual for individuals to spontaneously remember a past life as an animal. This is especially true if they came from cultures where the predominant religious belief is based on reincarnation and the transmigration of souls into animal bodies. It's also true for people who come from Earth-based cultures. It's very unusual for someone from our Western culture to recall a life as an animal in a past-life regression. I don't think this means that Westerners haven't had animal lives, whereas people from native cultures have; rather, I believe that since they live closer to the earth, native peoples are more in tune with the natural world and are more likely to *remember* past lives as animals.

Let me tell you a true story that gives credence to the idea of past lives as animals. As I previously mentioned, in my current life I lived in a Zen Buddhist monastery, and my years there were very austere. We were required to sit in meditation in the lotus or half-lotus position for up to 16 hours a day. During that time, we sat facing a bare wall inside the monastery. We weren't allowed to have our eyes open, for the Zen masters felt that we might be tempted to look around; however, we couldn't close our eyes either, for they felt that we might fall asleep or start visualizing rather than meditating. Instead, we were required to keep our eyes half open, in an unfocused gaze toward the wall. When we sat, our backs had to be ramrod straight, and we weren't permitted to move.

In these circumstances, it was easy to be distracted by pain or tiredness. So as an act of compassion, with lightning accuracy, the Zen master would strike the shoulder of a practitioner with a *kyosaku* stick to ensure attentiveness in his discipline. A *kyosaku* stick is similar to a flat baseball bat. The catch-22 of this practice was that if the Zen master deemed that you were doing well, he'd smack just as hard in order to encourage you!

In the quiet of the monastery, inner demons from our subconscious or from our past would rise into our awareness. This was disturbing and often took great courage to face. We were told by the Zen masters that no matter what we saw or experienced during our meditation, it was all an illusion and we must detach ourselves from it. I don't know if this is the best psychological way to deal with emotional difficulties, but this was how it was done in the Zen Buddhist tradition for hundreds of years, so we accepted it.

One of the most avid of the students at the monastery was a man named Chuck. One day, perhaps overwhelmed by the difficulty of the monastic practices, he committed suicide. After Chuck's death, something remarkable occurred.

While living at the monastery, I'd adopted a stray white cat. Shortly after Chuck's passing, the cat gave birth to six pure white kittens. One of the kittens had a blue eye and a green eye. Chuck had one blue eye and one green eye, too, but this seemed to be just a coincidence. In addition, the kitten fell from the roof of the garage and injured its leg, developing a limp. Chuck had walked with a limp, but this also seemed to be a coincidence. However, when all the kittens were old enough to be out chasing butterflies and scampering through the monastery gardens, we noticed something else very unusual.

Every time the gong was sounded to begin meditation, the kitten with the different-colored eyes would run to the door nearest to the meditation room. (Cats weren't allowed inside the monastery.) This solemn kitten would sit absolutely still outside the door for the entire lengthy meditation *as if in deep contemplation.* This occurred day after day and seemed abnormal for a young cat that would normally be active and playful. We couldn't help but wonder if that devoted being had been our friend Chuck. The kitten did seem attentive whenever we talked to her, and she particularly responded to the name that we gave her—*Chuckee.*

Chuck had been an awakened man, so perhaps after his death he didn't want to take the time to incarnate into a human body and go through all the effort of growing up. Maybe he came back in the cat's body to experience just a little of the physical world before going on to the next stage of his development.

Whether you've had a past life as an animal, have experienced life in an exalted position, or were forced to endure deep despair, when you can view your past lives in the larger context of reincarnation and karma, the many pieces of the puzzle—why you're here on Earth at this time in history and what your purpose is—will begin to fall into place.

Chapter Three

HOW PAST-LIFE EXPLORATION CAN HEAL YOUR LIFE

In order to heal and empower your present life, it's helpful to first know who and what you've been in previous incarnations. Past-life exploration (through regression) is a highly effective method for traveling deep into the inner recesses of your mind to the place where memories of all your prior existences are stored. It can be a direct path to the soul. As you uncover and heal old wounds from the past—and release self-limiting beliefs—you'll begin to understand your true purpose and place in the universe.

Is My Past Life Real?

When you embark on a regression, images and memories surface—sometimes in vivid detail. There are numerous documented cases of convincingly accurate details being recalled during past-life regressions, which are later validated through historical research. Participants of my seminars have also written to me and explained that they've investigated the lives that they *saw* during the group regression . . . and discovered that their visions were factual. However, most past lives haven't been recorded, so they've been lost forever, making it impossible to find written proof that your experiences before this lifetime were real.

You don't actually have to prove that your former lives are authentic—or even believe in reincarnation— to benefit from past-life therapy. Even my clients who were skeptical gained immense value from regressions. When a person's life transforms—as a result of witnessing images that emerge during deep meditation— healing has occurred. It's not important if those images are "true" past lives or not; the significance lies in the advantages you receive while exploring their meaning. Even if the mental pictures that come to the surface aren't past-life memories but are simply symbols from your subconscious, they deserve to be probed. They're legitimate expressions from your inner being, which can greatly increase the quality of your life.

Am I Making It Up?

When they discover a previous incarnation, participants in my past-life seminars sometimes say, "Am I just making this up?" I tell them to stop worrying about whether the images they see are real or not. The value lies in the results they achieve in their lives based on what they've learned from the regression—it's not about wondering if they're recalling a fantasy lifetime.

Although many of the memories you experience will be factual, proving their validity is a lot less important than the profound growth that can occur in your life just by viewing them. And on a spiritual level, of course you're making it up. Where do you think all of life came from? You're always "making it up," no matter what you're experiencing because the circumstances of your life come from the creative force within you. In no small way—in every moment—you're imagining and manifesting your life. So to remember your past lives, just let go and be willing to "make it up."

In our culture we're told to dismiss anything that doesn't fit within the normal consensus of reality. The reluctance to accept past-life memories may have its roots in our collective childhood . . . in which imagination was demeaned and relegated to the inconsequential world of make-believe. When children talk about an invisible friend or when someone sees a ghost or an angel, these individuals are told to ignore it, because it's "just their imagination." When people say, "Oh, that's just her imagination," and reduce its value in such a pejorative way, it's truly a desecration of one of our most sacred faculties—the ability to tap into our intuitive and visionary capacity.

Our imagination is one of the most powerful spiritual tools that we possess, for it's an entrance into other worlds and the pathway used by ancient seers to pierce into other dimensions and travel through time and space. Mystics and prophets also rely on it to traverse the subtle inner realm and access universal truths. It's a sacred ability of all human beings, so I invite you to awaken your creative spark and explore what and who you've been. Allow your imagination free rein without constantly questioning the images, and you'll begin to receive more accurate information regarding your previous lives. Remember that this faculty is a hallowed doorway to your far past.

Using Past-Life Exploration to Answer Important Questions about Your Life

Past-life journeys can sometimes provide the answers that traditional medicine or therapy can't. Of course there may be many contributing reasons for our problems—it can be all too easy to blame current difficulties on past-life behavior or actions. Nevertheless, exploration into earlier lives has proven to be incredibly powerful in many situations where other methods have failed. By knowing who we've been in previous lives, we can better understand our place and mission in the present. Life isn't a onetime affair, nor is it a series of meaningless experiences strung together. A journey backward in time will assist the process of gradually realizing our full potential as conscious, loving beings.

Your Health and Past Lives

Past-life regression can have a positive effect on all aspects of life and is especially beneficial for health problems. My client Karen came to me because she believed that she was sabotaging her own desire for a long-term, loving relationship; she also felt that she had a weight problem. Although there isn't necessarily a connection between body weight and relationships, Karen sensed that there *was* one for her. She was a 34-year-old, well-dressed woman and had about 30 pounds she couldn't lose. She was certain that her size was preventing her from experiencing a committed, satisfying relationship.

In a past-life journey, Karen vividly remembered a life as a prostitute in 18th-century England. She recalled the bitter cold of the London streets; the occasional frantic encounters with customers; and the long, hungry days. She was very unhappy in that life, and during her regression she relived her grief in being stuck in such a difficult profession. In addition, she got in touch with a belief that she had formed at the time: "If I'm attractive, men will desire me for my body, and I'll feel cheap and degraded."

She came into her current life with that statement embedded in her *bioenergy matrix*—her personal energy field. (Your energy field is made up of all the aspects of your other energetic systems, including your emotional body, astral body, and bioelectrical meridian system.) Beliefs, decisions, and judgments aren't just lodged in your brain; they also exist in your physical body and in the myriad energy fields that surround and penetrate your being.

In her regression, Karen discovered that even though she consciously wanted to feel attractive and desired, she was subconsciously afraid of being degraded again. This core belief had been controlling her life since she was a child. Anytime a man was attracted to her, she'd sabotage any chance of a relationship without even realizing it.

During our work together, she was able to release her old conviction, and her entire life changed as a result. She embraced a new principle about herself: *I can feel and be attractive. People are attracted to me for who I am— and who I am is wonderful.*

Almost immediately she started to lose those 30 pounds, but more important, she began to feel good about herself. Karen is now happily married and looking and feeling attractive. (I'll talk more about past-life resolution techniques in Chapter 8.)

I once worked with a young man named John who came to me for help in treating a physical problem he'd suffered with for many years. He couldn't perspire because his sweat glands didn't function properly, and as a result, his skin was dry, which was extremely uncomfortable. He'd tried numerous medications to no avail. He regressed to a time when he'd been a servant at a Russian court and was required to stand at attention for hours during banquets in case a guest beckoned. During one important occasion, he had a very full bladder but wasn't allowed to leave his post. Eventually he lost control and ran out of the banquet hall to relieve himself. In a subsequent fit of rage, his master killed him.

In the regression, John discovered a subconscious belief that he must hold back his bodily excretions or else die. His body translated this idea in such a way that he stopped perspiring. As soon as he discovered the source of his difficulty and resolved it, immediately (during the session) his sweat glands began to work. They've continued to do so ever since.

Your Relationships and Past Lives

Past-life regression can also help us understand relationships. A daughter who resents her mother telling her what to do may find that in a past life their roles were reversed—she was the domineering mother in a previous life, and vice versa. The resentful daughter may never have gotten over the feeling that *she* should be in charge, not the other way around. Remembering and understanding why she feels the way she does about her mother could help her create a healthier relationship in which she isn't being controlled by her past programming.

My client Sue had worked at the same job for seven years, and almost every day she was angry with her boss. He noticed every detail of her work and although he was kind, she felt that he was suffocating her. In her regression, Sue discovered a past life in which her current boss had been her husband—and he hadn't been attentive at all. In the 1800s, they'd been early settlers in Montana and lived in a small mountain cabin miles from any other habitation. In that life as a pioneer wife, Sue was very lonely and desired company. For weeks at a time, her husband would leave their cabin to go hunting and exploring. She used to complain that he wasn't attentive enough; and on one occasion when he was away, Sue was caught in a landslide behind the cabin and suffocated to death.

When she realized that her present boss was trying to make up for being inattentive in their past life together, she forgave him (while she was regressed) and also *released the subconscious need for his attention.* She also let him know that it wasn't his fault that she had suffocated. Even though she never told her boss about her regression, she remarked that from that day forward, he seemed completely changed. Even their colleagues noticed the difference. He was much more at ease with her, and everyone in the office enjoyed the benefits of his more relaxed mood.

Your Abundance and Past Lives

Whenever my client Mark started to get ahead financially, he'd back down from his success and wasn't quite able to make ends meet for his family. A common expression of Mark's was: "We're poor but we're happy." In a regression, he saw that he'd been a wealthy landowner in the Middle Ages. However, his family had been kidnapped and held for ransom by marauding bandits, and he never saw his young wife again (who also happened to be his wife in this life).

He recalled that in his past life, night after night he'd been slouched over in the damp quarters of his manor house, blaming himself and his wealth for the loss of his wife. This subconscious guilt had carried forward into his present life: He believed that if he had too much money, his family would be taken from him. This feeling was so strong that if he ever made enough money, he would have likely been separated from his family somehow *to support his subconscious belief.* After Mark recognized this thought pattern, a remarkable financial change occurred. He was quickly given a promotion since he was no longer sabotaging his advancement, and interestingly enough, he went into real estate. He and his family are now quite prosperous!

Past-Life Regressions to Activate Talents and Abilities

An exciting area of regression is the activation of past-life talents and abilities for use in one's present life. Rob came to one of my seminars and regressed to a time when he'd played the violin. The following week he bought a violin and began taking lessons. He reported that his teacher was astounded by how quickly and easily he was able to learn.

Carolyn had always wanted to sing but felt that she didn't have a good voice—she said that people used to tease her about it. After she regressed to a past life in which she'd been an excellent vocalist, she said that it seemed almost magical how dramatically her voice had improved. Now she sings in a choir in her hometown.

In my seminars, I often do a process specifically aimed at activating talents, abilities, and other beneficial qualities from previous lives. At the end of one of these exercises, a woman approached me and said, "I don't understand. In my past life, I saw that I was a shepherd. All I did every day was spend time in the hills by myself, occasionally herding sheep. What talent or ability is that?"

After spending a few minutes talking with her, she brought up the fact that she has six kids who keep her very busy. We realized that she tuned in to that particular past life so she could bring some inner peace and solitude into her current hectic life.

I've developed a technique in my seminars that seems to help bring a particular ability into the present time. Participants close their eyes as I help them reach a state of deep relaxation. While they experience a past life in which they exhibited special traits or talents, I ask them to move or position their body *as if* they were participating in their specific talent. For example, when Rob recalled a life as a violinist, I asked him to stand up (while his eyes remained closed) and move his arms and body just as if he were playing the violin. This process causes the body to remember how to perform the activity. Reenacting the motions—while experiencing a past life—actually helps to *implant* that special quality into your present physical body.

In one seminar when I was leading this talent process, I noticed a young man in the corner of the hall doing what looked like push-ups. I assumed that he must have been a good athlete in another life and was attempting to bring those athletic abilities into the present. During the break, I asked him what past-life talent he'd encountered. His face turned red, and he lowered his voice and whispered, "I was a great lover!" I can only hope that his lovemaking abilities have improved as a result of his sojourn into the past.

Releasing the Fear of Death

Another benefit of past-life regression is the release of the fear of death, which enables you to live more fully and with greater intensity. When you really comprehend the fact that you're infinite and eternal and *you* don't die when your body does, you begin to feel a deep inner peace that pervades your everyday activities.

The thought of dying can be frightening or extremely sad to someone who thinks that this one life is all there is. Mitchell had AIDS and was very seriously ill. He'd never possessed strong religious beliefs and was terrified of death. He didn't believe in reincarnation, but a friend persuaded him to consult me. I told him that he didn't have to believe in reincarnation—instead, he and I could do a past-life process and call the images he saw "soul dramas." I explained that the snapshot images he would experience were a valid expression of his subconscious mind—whether they were previous lives or symbolic representations of his psyche wasn't important—and those inner messages deserved to be heard, no matter where they came from. He could accept that point of view.

Mitchell went into a deeply relaxed state very quickly, as images and feelings of other times and places came easily to him. Suddenly he had a spontaneous encounter seemingly unsolicited by anything I said. He saw all the bodies that he'd inhabited in every one of his lifetimes coming forward like a great gathering of friends. Some were male and some were female, and many races were represented as well. As he stood in the center of this group, one of these past selves came forward and told him what he had gained from each life. Eventually, a body that looked exactly like his present one also stepped forward and said, "Each life allows you a greater and deeper understanding of who you are in your entirety. Each life is special, important, and valuable. The body that you currently inhabit is allowing you to develop your ability to receive love. You're learning this lesson well, and soon you'll be going home."

At this point Mitchell began to sob, as the dam of uncertainty, fear, and pain crumbled. When he gained composure, he smiled and said, "I've never felt such a deep sense of peace. I'm ready to go when it's my time." He died a few weeks later, but I was told that his last moments of life were filled with profound grace and serenity.

Why Past-Life Regression Works

Past-life regression is healing because it allows you to get to the source of your problems; until then, you're dealing with symptoms rather than causes. The philosopher George Santayana said, "Those who cannot remember the past are condemned to repeat it." In other words, when you release yourself from the limitations of the past, you can be free. Whether you call it genetic coding, cellular memory, or even collective unconsciousness, we're all ruled by the vast repository of our previous experiences; and in many ways, they dictate the situations we encounter in the present.

For example, many compulsions and phobias are rooted in the distant past. If you've always hated wearing anything tight around your neck, you may discover that you were choked to death in a previous lifetime. By reliving—and healing—ancient memories and associated emotions, your current life-limiting behaviors will change.

We often create incidents today that subconsciously remind us of events from our former lives in an attempt to heal the original pain. If emotions such as fear, anger, or grief were suppressed during traumatic events in a past life, they'll stay embedded in your energy field and form inner conflicts that recur lifetime after lifetime. As you continue to push these undesired feelings deeper into your psyche, a greater barrier builds between you and whatever you're afraid to confront. But when you relive a past-life incident, the emotions and decisions that were held back for so long finally have the opportunity to rise to the surface and be released so that they no longer control you.

To understand why past-life therapy works, it's important to realize that it's not necessarily what you endured in your earlier lives that creates problems in your present life; rather, it's the trauma and emotions that you *suppressed* in the past that initiates difficulties in the present. Your past experiences don't cause continuing problems—it's your *reactions* to them that create challenges. For example, falling into a ravine in a former life won't necessarily create a blockage in your present life, but tumbling down while feeling suppressed intense emotional anguish could.

Joshua experienced a past life as a young man in medieval Europe. He remembered telling his trusted friends at the time that contrary to the accepted belief, he strongly felt that the king wasn't directly descended from God. Furious, his friends chased after him, causing him to fall down a ravine. As he fell, he was in turmoil—he loved his friends, yet that feeling was at odds with his fear as they brutally pursued him. As he plummeted, he made a decision that he'd never again share his feelings honestly.

In Joshua's present life, he had always been afraid to speak his mind. In fact, when he'd start to say what he really felt, he'd often physically trip or stumble. He'd developed a subconscious association between speaking his mind and actually falling, but it wasn't the physical trauma of his accident that caused his present-day blockage—it was the tumultuous emotions he felt at the time that he fell. Joshua was eventually able to change his lifelong pattern by using past-life resolution techniques. Now he's confident in his current life and can communicate what he really feels without fear.

Imagine two similar scenarios. In the first, an Aztec warrior is fighting alongside his best friend. The dust is churning as spears fly on either side of the gallant warrior. Suddenly in the haze of battle, a spear is flung straight at the chest of his friend. The young warrior steps in front of it, valiantly saving the life of his comrade. Mortally wounded by the spear that pierced his chest, he dies but feels a deep peace, for he has saved his friend's life.

In the second scenario, two young warriors are battling side by side. They are best friends. Suddenly in the thrall of battle and obscured by thick haze and dust, one turns to the other and thrusts a spear into his friend's chest. As the warrior lies dying on the battlefield, he learns that his best friend is having an affair with his wife and wants him out of the way. He dies making a decision that he can never really trust anyone.

In both scenes the physical trauma is the same— a spear wound to the chest causes death. In the first instance, the Aztec warrior feels exhilaration at having spared the life of his friend. In the second scenario, however, the warrior decides that it's unwise to trust anyone. In future lives, whenever this man begins to get close to someone, similar memories and decisions will be activated. Whenever he starts to trust, he experiences severe chest pains and the fear of being betrayed. For him, establishing a bond with another activates an emotional *and* physical response from a past life.

It's not your past-life trauma that causes your present-day blockages; it's the <u>meaning</u> you give to those events that haunts you through time. And it's possible to travel back and change the significance of any event, and thus create a time/space domino effect that transforms your present life.

The Role of the Subconscious in Past-Life Exploration

Maybe you've heard the expression: *You are what you think.* This idea refers not simply to what you *know* you think, but more important, to what you *don't know* you think. For example, you may be unaware that beliefs lie deep inside your subconscious making you feel unworthy and undeserving of success, which sets up inner blocks to fulfillment and creates frustration. Your subconscious mind exerts a far greater control over your life than you can possibly realize. It literally directs your reality. Imagine a plane flying straight toward a mountainside in the fog. The control tower (the conscious mind) could be yelling, "Turn back! Turn back!" But unless the subconscious mind (the pilot) gets the message, the plane will crash.

People often wonder why our minds accept self-defeating programming in the first place. After all, don't we desire the very best for ourselves? Don't we all really want to be healthy, happy, and successful? The answers to these questions lie in the nature of the subconscious mind. Although your consciousness has the ability to reason and decide what's best for you, it can't implement any decision unless the subconscious mind agrees. A woman who overeats may want to give up the habit, yet she'll continue to do so despite her conscious mind's desperate attempts to stop. The subconscious acts as it has been programmed, in much the same way as a computer functions.

For example, a mother might say to her young son, "You're so clumsy! You've got no rhythm and will never be able to dance." The child's critical faculties aren't developed enough to reject this negative input, so he may grow up being clumsy and unrhythmic because the subconscious has accepted the idea as fact. In other words, awkwardness and lack of dexterity had been programmed into the subconscious mind. This then becomes an integral part of the child's self-image. As an adult, he might reason that he doesn't need to be clumsy and with enough training he'll be able to dance. However, if the conscious mind proposes a belief that's different from the subconscious programming, the subconscious mind will always be dominant.

The subconscious mind is also of great importance to our survival. For example, if a barking dog bit you when you were four years old, you probably have a programmed fear of barking dogs. As an adult, if you came upon an aggressive dog—even a small one leashed to a heavy chain—you'd likely feel a momentary spasm of panic because the initial fear had been ingrained in you to protect and ensure your survival. Your conscious mind may know that you're safe, but the programming is so strongly embedded in the subconscious that you instinctively respond with fear.

Your subconscious mind accepts programming not only from early childhood, but also from past lives. For example, I had a client who was so terrified of bees that she became almost paralyzed whenever she saw one. She'd been stung to death by bees in a past life, so her subconscious mind—wanting to ensure her survival—made a decision to avoid bees. Even though the conscious mind thinks, *It's just a little bee; you're much bigger and stronger,* the subconscious thoughts take precedence.

The subconscious mind is so powerful that beliefs from early childhood and past lives become *glued* into your energy field and coalesce into form in the physical world. For example, if you have a core thought that all your romances will fail, you'll continue to create relationships that fall apart—even though consciously you want one that will be enduring and loving. Past-life therapy works by reaching deep into your inner wellspring and reprogramming the old beliefs and decisions that are influencing every aspect of your life.

No Victims—Just Volunteers

When you connect with a past life—either through dreams, regression, or in waking consciousness—it's important to remember that there are no victims . . . just volunteers. Every experience you've had may have been a necessary part of your spiritual growth to get you to the point where you are now. Please keep this in mind, especially when you encounter a lifetime in which you were a victim (or a tyrant).

I imagine the victim-volunteer scenario going something like this: You're walking around in the spirit world. You've examined your past lives and decide that for your next incarnation, it would be valuable to learn humility in order to further your evolution.

You begin to pull aside passing spirits. "Hey, I'm about to incarnate. Why don't you incarnate, too, and teach me some humility?"

The spirits all shy away from you, saying, "No way! I'm not going to mess up my karmic evolution by helping you achieve humility."

Then finally shuffling up to the pearly gates comes Harry, an old acquaintance. You've shared lifetime after lifetime together—you love him deeply on a soul level.

"Hey, Harry, I really need to learn humility. How about it?" And Harry shrugs, lovingly puts his arm around you, and agrees.

He replies, "Only because I love you so much will I do this, because you know that it will be hard for both of us."

You thank Harry profusely for the depth of his love and leap out of the spirit world into a baby's body—and Harry, in turn, does the same. Gradually you both grow up, and Harry becomes your boss at your new job. It seems like he's victimizing you, and you hate him with every ounce of your being. (You forget that you begged him to incarnate with you.) But along the way, you learn humility.

The individuals who victimized you are usually the very ones who love you the most deeply on a soul level. In my regression work, I've discovered time and time again that after processing the grief, rage, and bitterness that we hold against our abusers, there's almost always an enormous well of love that's uncovered.

Forgiving Past-Life Circumstances

One of the most powerful things that you can gain from past-life therapy is forgiveness. In order to heal, you must be willing to forgive the past. It's much easier to pardon those who have hurt you in your present life once you understand the karma that precipitated the situation. When you travel to the past-life source of your hurt—to absolve yourself and others—a loving energy weaves its way through time and space to your current life. Of course it's important to forgive those who hurt or denied you in a previous lifetime; however, it's just as vital to release the guilt for things that you did to others. (If you have difficulty letting go, you must forgive yourself for *not* forgiving.)

When people regress to a past life, they often realize that everything that ever happened to them was necessary for their soul's growth and development. In fact, they realize that without those experiences, they wouldn't be who they are today. The place beyond forgiveness is acceptance—total, unconditional acceptance, without judging yourself or anyone else. I find this one of the most healing aspects of past-life regression therapy.

I'm often asked if my past-life explorations have allowed me to discover why I was so brutally shot. Yes, I've found some satisfactory answers. Using this technique, I came to understand my karmic connection with my attacker, and this has enabled me to forgive him.

I realized that I shared a life with him in China. All the people in our small village lived in homes that were built up off the ground, and the villagers placed bodily waste through holes in the floor that dropped into containers underneath the houses. Every morning a man (the one who shot me) came and cleared away the waste beneath the houses. He was more or less an "untouchable," who had no social standing in the community. Though my disdain for him in that life was a minor thing to me, it was significant to him. And in this life, shooting me was of slight concern to him but was a major incident for me. (It's believed that he had killed a number of women.) We had a slight yet intense karmic connection. I'd never seen him in my present life before I was shot, and I saw him only once more—at the trial.

When I discovered my past-life connection with this man, I finally understood the significance of my last thought before he pulled the trigger: *He's aiming too low!* I had a subconscious desire to balance the karma of having treated him cruelly in that past life. (If he had aimed any higher, he would have killed me.) Through discovering my past connection with this individual, I was able to forgive him and accept what had happened, thus releasing any resentment that could be carried into my present relationships.

Some of the most rewarding comments I receive after past-life seminars relate to forgiving present and past-life circumstances. In Australia, I conducted a seminar at the Japanese-owned Nikko Hotel, and a woman who attended that seminar later wrote me an interesting letter. Upon entering the hotel, she experienced an intense wave of resentment and panic washing over her and thought, *I can't attend this seminar in this hotel.* She almost fled but was very glad that she stayed because a debilitating condition, which she'd had since she was a teenager, totally healed.

In her letter, she told me that when she was 17 years old, she had been taken prisoner in Indonesia by Japanese soldiers during World War II. She wrote: "I suffered physically as well as mentally from their brutality during the rest of the war. I survived, but my intestines were damaged from untreated dysentery. I was severely undernourished, and I harbored a deep hatred for everything Japanese. This has continued ever since. I've sought treatment from many physicians and psychologists during the last 50 years, but I've had to live with a chronic weakness of the bowel and a constant pain in the solar plexus."

She had come to see her suffering as something that she carried for all reviled people in the world. She continued: "Whenever I see or read about instances of brutality and inhumanity against others—especially children—the pain becomes almost unbearable."

The woman went on to tell me that after she'd regressed to a past life in my seminar, she was able to observe the source of her current resentment (she didn't mention what the past life was). As a result of forgiving prior-life circumstances, the pain that had plagued her for 50 years had completely lifted! "My debilitating pain disappeared during the seminar, and today I'm still free of it! When I left the hotel, I even gave a friendly greeting to the Japanese staff," she wrote. She added that she had spent time talking to some of them and found them to be very pleasant, lovely people: "I feel free! Free from pain! Free from all animosity and all resentment! Truly and gloriously free and easy!"

Another seminar participant, Gerald, had a vicious relationship with his brother in his current life. As they were growing up, their mother was concerned that the brothers might kill each other because they fought so ferociously. The animosity had continued into adulthood and was causing great upheaval for the entire family. In addition, Gerald felt that his hatred was taking up so much of his energy that it was preventing him from being successful.

Gerald regressed to a life in 16th-century Scandinavia, where he and his present-day brother had been rivals for the same woman. He remembered that on a cold, snowy afternoon they'd fought over this woman, but neither had won her hand because they'd both died from their injuries. In his present life, he was creating a similar scenario. When he truly forgave his rival in his past-life regression, he described it as if a huge weight had been lifted from his shoulders. He told me that it seemed like a miracle because the next time he saw his brother, he felt only love and compassion for him. For the first time in their lives, they sat down together and truly shared from their hearts. Gerald said that it was a turning point for him, and he's now beginning to succeed in his career as well as heal the lifelong hurt and resentment that he harbored against his brother.

We Don't Know the Whole Story

To help you understand and forgive what individuals may have done to you—and what you've done to others—in your past lives, here's a story I'd like to share with you that I often tell in my seminars. My Chinese tai chi teacher told me that it's an ancient Chinese story, my Sufi teacher swears that it's an age-old Sufi story, and a wise friend from India has declared that it's originally from India. So since there's some disagreement about its origins, I give it a Native American flavor—in alignment with *my* ancestry.

A long time ago, an old man lived in a tepee in a Native American village. He had an extremely beautiful horse. All the people in the villages across the plains spoke of this remarkable horse—a magnificent animal with a glorious sheen and muscles that rippled with every movement.

The Great Chief sent a messenger on horseback to the old man to ask if he could purchase it. The warrior messenger raced to the old man's tepee and jumped down from his horse.

"Old man, I'm here on behalf of the Great Chief. He sends his greetings and asks that he may buy your horse."

The old man had gentle dignity and quiet manners, and he remained silent for a long time. Finally he spoke and said, "Please give my regards to the Great Chief and thank him for his kind offer to buy my horse. However, this horse is my friend. We are companions. I know his soul, and I feel that he knows mine—I can't sell my friend."

The messenger nodded briefly in acknowledgment, mounted his horse, and rode away. Two weeks later, the old man's horse disappeared.

When the villagers heard that the horse was missing, they all gathered around the old man. "Oh, old man, this is very bad fortune! You could have sold your horse to the Great Chief, but now you have no horse and no payment. What bad fortune!"

The old man replied, "It's not bad or good. We don't know the whole story. Let's just say that the horse is gone."

The villagers went away shaking their heads because they knew that this was bad luck. However, a month later the old man's horse returned, followed by 20 other magnificent horses. Each one was spirited and bursting with vitality and exuberance. The villagers ran to the old man and exclaimed, "You were right! It wasn't bad fortune that your horse ran away—it was good fortune. Now not only do you have your horse back, but you have 20 more beautiful horses. This is good fortune!"

The old man slowly shook his head and with utmost compassion said, "It's not good or bad. We don't know the whole story. Let's just say that the horse has returned."

The people went away shaking their heads. They knew that it was very good fortune to have so many beautiful horses. The old man had one son, who started to break the horses. Every day he would wake up early to continue his work. One morning the old man came to watch his son, who had a natural grace as he swung onto the bare back of a wild pinto. The horse bucked violently to the left and twisted to the right. Suddenly with a ferocious kick of his hind legs, the pinto tossed the young man high in the air. He landed in a crumpled heap in the dust, and both his legs were broken.

All the inhabitants of the village gathered, with great moaning and commiserating. "Oh no! Oh no! Old man, your horse returning to you was very bad fortune. Now your only son has both legs broken and is crippled. Who's going to take care of you? This is very bad fortune."

The old man pulled himself upright and with respect replied, "It's not bad fortune; it's not good fortune. Just say my son broke his legs, for we don't know the whole story." Once again the villagers walked away shaking their heads—they knew it was very bad fortune.

Then war broke out across the land and the Great Chief called all the young men in the villages to battle. It was an untimely war and the villagers knew that they'd never see their sons again. Once more they gathered around the old man. "Old man, you're right. It's not bad fortune that your son broke his legs because even though he's crippled, you have your son. We'll never see our sons again. It was good fortune for you."

And once again the old man said, "It's not good fortune; it's not bad fortune. We don't know the whole story."

✣

As you explore your past lives, there will be times when you'll experience the role of the victim and the victimizer. Step beyond right and wrong, and resist passing judgment. Who you've been and what you've experienced in the past isn't good . . . and it isn't bad. *You might not know the whole story.*

Every experience that you've ever had—everything that's been done to you and everything that you've done to others—has been necessary for your spiritual evolution. Even the lies that you told or occasions when you were cruel or unjust have been important. The shameful things that reside in your soul have helped you become who you are. *All* of your experiences have been an important part of your soul's journey. To the extent that you can forgive and accept yourself exactly as you are, you become a more powerful force for healing on the planet. Remember, *It's not good. It's not bad. You don't know the whole story.*

Releasing Guilt from the Past

In the mid-1970s, I took a trip to Italy. One morning I got up early to hike up a hill and watch the sun rise. As the first rays of light broke over the horizon, I was overwhelmed with deep sadness accompanied by a powerful vision. In my mind's eye as I looked upon the valley, I was "seeing" not a 20th-century scene but another time. I could see smoke rising from numerous small campfires and mixing with the morning mist. No one was up yet. As I stood on that hill, I knew that I'd been there before as the Roman commander of a large army that had been fighting for a long time.

Asleep by the campfires, there weren't just men present but also women and even some children. I felt wave after wave of grief fill me, for I knew that this would be our last battle. Rather than surrender, I made the decision that we'd fight on that day. I knew that I'd have to speak to the troops with conviction about our victory . . . but I also knew that it was the day of our deaths. I realized that we would be killed without mercy, but the alternatives were imprisonment, starvation, or slavery for my people. What might I have done differently? These were my people. I loved them. Perhaps if I'd been a better leader, we wouldn't be facing imminent death.

These questions were superimposed on my present-day consciousness that morning. Twenty years later, that experience in Italy was only a wisp of a memory. I was leading a reincarnation seminar in New Zealand, and one of the organizers had brought her young son along to help her. Unbeknownst to me, the boy decided to participate in one of the past-life processes (as a rule, I don't think children should be regressed until they're at the age of consent).

During the break, he came up to me and said with soft sadness, "Denise, do you remember when we were Romans? Do you remember when we were on a hillside watching the smoke rise from the campfires from the night before, and we were preparing for the big battle?"

To my amazement, this child—who had no way of knowing about my experience in Italy—spoke with quiet certainty of the battle that took place that day.

A year later, a man who had also never heard of my experience on that hillside said, "Denise, do you remember when we were together in Italy as Roman soldiers?

You were the commander, and I fought alongside you at the last battle. It was magnificent—we all fought so gallantly. It was one of the most powerful experiences of all my lifetimes."

I was astounded! He not only remembered the same life, but he felt exhilarated by it. It was a profound lesson for me to see that I didn't always know the *whole* story. I'd felt culpable for causing the deaths of so many people, and I'd taken responsibility for the experiences of others and had even presumed to know what those situations entailed. But now I could see that I no longer needed to carry that blame, and I also realized that my guilty feelings were arrogant—I was only accountable for my own experience and actions.

All of us manifest the necessary situations that are valuable for our growth. I didn't need to continue to shoulder guilt for everyone else, for we *all* jointly created the landscape for that last battle. This might sound like a subtle realization, but for me it made a huge difference. Until then I'd feel responsible for just about everything—even for things over which I had no control. If you told me that you had dented your car by backing into a post—as strange as it sounds—most likely *I* would have felt guilty. To finally begin releasing this emotion was incredibly freeing.

It's not uncommon to feel this way about a disturbing past life, but it's important to remember that there's never any reason to assume guilt for past-life experiences that you encounter. When you do so, you're not taking responsibility for yourself. Guilt is a way of saying, "I really didn't do it. It really isn't my fault." Acknowledge all your actions without judgment. If you've hurt someone, make it right; if you've acted inappropriately, alter your behavior. But don't dishonor the situation, the other person, or yourself by feeling guilty.

Whenever the pain of guilt seems to attract you, remember this: If you yield to it instead of forgiving yourself, you're deciding against inner peace. Therefore, say to yourself gently but with conviction: *I accept who I am and what I've done as well as what others have done to me. I accept and forgive myself.*

One valuable technique is to write down all your feelings of guilt. After you've done so, burn the pages and say, "I release now and forever my attachments to this guilt. So be it." This may help you begin the process of letting go.

In your far past, you've experienced a variety of lives and may have been a feudal lord, mystic, martyr, slave, slave master, saint, beggar, or king . . . the list is as endless as the history of humanity. And every past life that you've weathered—no matter how violent, depressing, bleak, or wasted—has given you a chance to recognize and release old patterns and heal ancient karma. Each life has furthered your journey into the depths of the soul and ultimately is bringing you closer to the profound and transcendent reality of the Creator.

Chapter Four

TRACKING CLUES . . . BECOMING A PAST-LIFE DETECTIVE

*"Through analysis of your present strong
tendencies you can pretty accurately
surmise what kind of life you led before."*
— Paramahansa Yogananda, from *Man's Eternal Quest*

Discovering who you were in a past life can be easy
and fun! There are a number of methods you can employ,
and in this chapter you'll learn how to uncover amazing
evidence of your previous lives *without ever doing a regression.* When you examine the present, you can pick up
hundreds of clues that can help you glean information
from the past. After you read the following section—and

before advancing to the past-life regression processes—I strongly recommend that you take the Past-Life Clues Questionnaire in the next chapter. This is a powerful way to open the door for spontaneous past-life recall, without requiring you to go into an altered state of consciousness. You might even think of yourself as a *past-life detective* as you amass clues from your affinities and experiences in your current life.

No single factor can provide all the answers, but if you gather them together, you can begin to solve the puzzle of who you might have been in previous incarnations. Here's a list of the areas of your life that we'll explore in more detail:

- Childhood games
- Childhood preferences and inclinations
- Clothing styles
- Architecture and home-furnishing styles
- Food preferences and eating habits
- Allergies
- Geographical locations
- Climates
- Cultures
- Time periods or historical events
- Music
- Scents, aromas, and smells
- Déjà vu experiences
- Talents and abilities
- Occupations and hobbies
- Heritage and ancestry
- Your name
- Books and films
- Animals and pets
- Personality traits, mannerisms, and habitual behaviors

- Relationships
- Causes you're passionate about
- Traumatic events
- Fears and phobias
- Words and phrases you use
- Body type
- Health issues
- Scars, birthmarks, and tattoos
- Injuries, diseases, and surgeries
- Dreams

Childhood Games

The most common childhood games are the result of programming by society. For example, a young girl is given a baby doll and is told that she's its mother. Her games of playing "Mom" to her baby are, in part, conditioned by her culture. Other kids' games are the result of a child symbolically imitating or acting out the behavior of adults. A young boy might observe his father doing repairs around the house, and he'll then fashion a makeshift hammer and pretend he's making bookshelves. Sometimes, however, playtime activities are a residue of memories from earlier lives. As you examine the games that you instinctively played, look for possible reflections that could have originated in the distant past.

For example, I had a friend who as a child used to make a prisonlike structure out of cardboard; then she'd climb inside it and pretend she was starving. She even got her friends to "sneak" small pieces of stale bread to her. When my friend was an adult, she spontaneously remembered living in a concentration camp. As soon as she recalled that event, she understood why she had played that game over and over again as a child—she was reenacting a significant experience from a past life.

Here's another example: As a child, Chantal used to persuade her friends to lie down and act like they were wounded. She then painted various parts of their bodies with red paint to simulate blood and asked her "patients" to moan. She'd rip up her mother's rags to make bandages, and sometimes she'd even pretend to amputate someone's limb that was "too far gone." In her past-life regression, Chantal recalled being a doctor on the battlefields of France during the Napoleonic Wars; her childhood game echoed that previous lifetime.

When I was six, I used to explore the woods by our house and would spend hours alone picking small bits of different plants and tasting them. I'd bring a bunch of my selections home, let them dry, and then attempt to grind the dried plants into powder. I called my concoctions "medicine" and would try to get my friends to take some if they weren't feeling well. I now believe that this activity was based on my memories as a Blackfoot Indian, gathering medicinal herbs for my tribe.

A skeptic might say this behavior could have been the result of being influenced by stories I'd heard or information that I'd subconsciously absorbed from my mom or dad. But my parents never used herbs and neither did my Cherokee grandparents. Why would a six-year-old fixate on one particular activity to the exclusion of all others? There can be many reasons, and one answer is that it can be traced to a previous life.

And how does a skeptical individual explain a child who's a master musician even though his or her parents aren't musically talented? Although it's impossible to prove beyond a doubt that reincarnation occurs, it's enormously valuable to observe childhood games, for they often hold important keys to understanding past lives.

Childhood Preferences and Inclinations

The younger the child, the more potent past-life memories usually are. My grandmother told me that when I was three, I'd get very irritated with her because she didn't remember our previous life together. She said that I'd plaintively ask again and again, "Don't you remember when we were sisters?"

When my daughter, Meadow, was three, she used to talk about her servants. I found this rather curious, considering that we maintained a casual lifestyle and often ate our meals seated on the floor. (This could probably be traced to my Native American life, sitting and eating by the fire.) However, even as a three-year-old, Meadow insisted on sitting at the table and would place numerous spoons, forks, and knives neatly next to her plate, as if in a formal dinner setting. Then she'd ask me to arrange the food on her plate into a beautiful presentation. This ritual was very important to her and was completely different from our brown-rice-with-vegetables lifestyle.

She'd also request that I place her clothes on the bed. She'd plead, "My servants used to lay my clothes out for me. I don't know how to dress myself." When her friends came over, Meadow would organize genteel games along with elaborate tea parties. One day they went outside to play, and I encouraged her to join them.

She responded gravely, "I'm not allowed to play outdoors with other children. I must not soil my clothes."

The pain and sadness of a lonely royal had seemingly filtered down into her childhood games.

Children's attitudes can often be attributed to their environment or upbringing, but I don't think this is the case for Meadow, as my husband and I are relaxed and informal. Meadow continues to be quite the lady; however, I can't help but think that she chose us as parents in order to balance a past life that was extremely traditional and rigid.

Asking family members what you were like as a child can also be helpful. One of my friends told me that one day, many years ago, she was driving in her car with her four-year-old daughter and when they drove over a bridge, the little girl casually said, "These are the killing waters."

Shocked, my friend asked her daughter what she meant, and she proceeded to tell her mom that she had drowned in the water below when she and her "other brother" were swimming, and her "other mother" was very sad. My friend, who had no interest in reincarnation at the time, researched local papers and discovered that more than 30 years earlier, a brother and sister had been swimming at that exact spot . . . and the young girl had drowned. (As my friend's daughter grew older, she lost all memories of this event.)

Clothing Styles

Valuable clues to your past lives can often be found in the types of clothing you're drawn to (or that you detest). For example, if you prefer long, flowing scarves and soft, loose fabrics (and you love the tall, stately stone pillars of

Greek architecture), you might have spent a previous life in ancient Greece. Of course there can be many reasons why you enjoy those particular styles, but as you begin to assemble clues, your aesthetic preferences can be very helpful in understanding the whole picture.

Are you attracted to gypsy, peasant, or military fashions? Does a specific ethnic style appeal to you? Do you enjoy wearing long dresses or dinner jackets, or do you loathe formal wear and just like to feel comfortable? Are there certain types of hats that you've worn regularly? I knew an American man who donned a Greek-style cap every day; he discovered that he'd been a Greek sailor in a past life. A French man I knew who always wore a cowboy hat found that he was once a cowboy in the 19th-century Wild West. An Australian woman with a penchant for berets realized that she'd been in the French Resistance during World War II.

The colors of clothing may also have past-life significance. For example, I knew a woman who always appeared in saffron yellow garments—it was more or less her trademark. During a regression, she recalled being a Hindu monk in India, wearing saffron-colored robes daily.

Architecture and Home-Furnishing Styles

Examine the architectural styles that you admire. Are you fascinated by Tudor, Georgian, or Victorian designs; or are you interested in structures such as cabins, tepees, yurts, cliff dwellings, or perhaps even castles and Greek temples? What do you like and dislike?

Caitlin had a fascination with yurts and managed to live in a number of them. She understood her passion when she regressed to a life in Mongolia, where she and her family had lived in a yurt. Charles loved castles so much that after he retired he constructed a façade for his home, giving it castle-like features. In a past life in Austria, he remembered being a mason who actually worked on those impressive fortresses. During that time, he always wished that he could be the one who lived in the castle, instead of the laborer who built it. So his passion filtered through to his current life.

Your home furnishings are another kind of clue into your past. Is one of your rooms decked out like a Bedouin tent? If so, this might be indicative of a lifetime spent in Northern Africa. Does your home resemble a cottage in England? Perhaps you once lived in the English countryside. Terra's home was decorated in Asian style. Each room was filled with Eastern adornments; and she had numerous statues of Buddha, bamboo flooring, and even wallpaper made from rice. When I entered her home, I almost felt like I'd stepped into a Zen monastery; in fact, Terra regressed to a life in which she'd been the gardener of a Zen temple in Japan. (Her own garden in this lifetime was very Zen-like in appearance.)

Another thing to examine is your relationship to your home. Do you tend to move often? This can indicate a prior experience of living a nomadic lifestyle. Do you want to stay in one house forever? This points to a past life where you were born and lived your entire life in one residence. Alternatively, this could also signify a previous incarnation as a refugee who always longed to have a permanent home.

Food Preferences and Eating Habits

Your childhood associations around eating and food preparation can often be indicative of past lives. As I mentioned earlier, when Meadow was a very small child, she always insisted that multiple forks and spoons be laid next to her plate for every meal. This was an energy echo from a past life of luxury. When he was a small boy, Tommy used to sit and balance his lunch on his knee as he hunched down in a hole that he'd dug in his backyard. There was almost nothing his mother could do to persuade him to eat at the table. As an adult, he regressed to a life during World War I when he used to eat in his dugout during battles. Kerry had a habit that frightened her family, as she always wanted to eat raw meat. It was only when she traveled back to an earlier life as an Eskimo, in which this was a standard dietary practice, that she realized where this particular behavior originated. Another woman, as a child, would only eat with one of her hands and had to be forced to use silverware. She later discovered that she had a past life in the Middle East where she ate using just her fingers.

Sometimes the types of food that you're attracted to as an adult can offer previous-life clues. If asked to pick what you enjoy the most, would you choose Indian, Chinese, Thai, Japanese, French, Italian, Greek, African, Spanish, Mexican, English, Scandinavian, German, Russian, Vietnamese, Hungarian, or some other ethnic cuisine? What cooking style or ingredients do you prefer? For example, if you really love pineapples and papayas, this might indicate that you once lived in a tropical climate. If you're passionate about pickled herring, perhaps in a previous life you incarnated in Scandinavia.

How you consume your meals can also offer important clues. Do you eat like a peasant? King? Monk? Samurai? Andrea always recited a prayer before every meal, and she felt that it was a sacrilege not to do so. She soon discovered that this habit came from a life as a Catholic monk in Italy in which no one was allowed to eat until prayers were said.

Allergies

Are you allergic to particular foods? Food allergies can, of course, come from many sources, but I've had clients who discovered that theirs had origins in past lives. Alison had an unusual physical reaction to chicken that could be traced to a previous life in Scotland. At the turn of the last century, as a child, she had been forced to eat her pet chicken. As soon as she released the trauma around that event, her allergic reaction disappeared.

Additionally, allergies of all kinds may sometimes have their sources in the past. For example, Peter reacted badly to all kinds of wine, but when he regressed to a life in Hungary and saw that he'd died of alcoholism caused by ingesting too much wine, he was able to heal. Grace, another client, was allergic to paper products. She uncovered a life spent working at a printing press in the 1800s in which she slowly died of exposure from the toxic inks that were used. (It's interesting to note that although she died from contact with the poisonous ink, she associated her suffering with the paper that was around her; so in a subsequent life, Grace developed an aversion to paper products, rather than to ink.)

It's not uncommon for an allergy to flare up at the exact same age that you were in a past life when a traumatic event occurred. For example, when Sam was 22, he suddenly developed an allergic reaction to gasoline. In a past-life regression, he remembered being a young man *at age 22* in England in the 1940s, and his job was to fuel airplanes.

When one of the airplanes that he'd just worked on exploded upon takeoff, he associated the trauma of that event with the smell of the gasoline he was inhaling at the time of the accident. Even though it wasn't his fault, he'd felt responsible. In his present life when he was 22 years old, one of his friends died in a fiery car crash. Again, although it wasn't his fault—he wasn't even there—that disaster released feelings of guilt and also sparked the onset of an allergy to gasoline.

Geographical Locations

An excellent exercise to activate past-life memories is to imagine yourself in a variety of terrains. Immerse all of your senses . . . sights, sounds, scents, textures, and so on as you imagine each environment. What feeling does each locale evoke within you? Be open to every nuance of your experience, as this will often trigger memories from your far past. When Peggy tried this exercise, she found that every time she imagined being surrounded by snowcapped mountains, she felt immensely happy. She discovered that this was consistent with a previous life in which she'd owned goats and resided in the mountains of Switzerland. One of my other clients, Carl, realized that his lifelong repulsion toward India had its source in an unhappy lifetime living in a northern region of the country.

Climates

Although you might think that almost everyone would prefer a temperate climate, it's surprising how much variety there is in people's weather preferences. A strong emotional response to specific conditions often has its source in a past life. For example, Heather loved and felt comforted by overcast days, but she didn't understand why she felt this way until she regressed to a previous happy life spent in London. She realized that she associated the cloudy skies with the joy she experienced during that lifetime.

Samuel, who lived in a farming community in Iowa, loved steamy hot climates. Even as a child, he asked his mom to paint a jungle scene in his bedroom. Samuel told me that sometimes he'd run the hot water in the bathroom to fill the room with steam, and he'd feel completely at home there. In his past-life regression, he recalled living in a humid rain forest—a lush jungle where monkeys flew effortlessly through the treetops.

Cultures

Carefully examining the cultures that you're interested in can offer you a pathway back in to your past. Jason had a fascination with Egyptian civilization. Even as a child, his most prized possession was an ankh that his uncle brought him from a vacation to Egypt. His interest grew as a teen, and he read books about the country and also did a senior-class project on the great pyramids. As an adult, Jason visited museum exhibits of Egyptian artifacts. He wasn't surprised when he discovered a past life in Egypt.

Time Periods or Historical Events

One early morning, I was walking through the woods in the Cascade Mountains in Washington State. As I hiked over a hill, I saw old-fashioned canvas tents in the mist-covered valley below. Each tent had a campfire in front of it, as the lingering smoke from the previous night's fire slowly spiraled upward and mixed with the early morning mist. (It's amazing how similar in feeling this was to the "vision" I had in Italy while standing on the hill.) As I watched, men wearing gray Confederate Civil War uniforms staggered out of their tents and began to prepare their morning meal.

I'm a bit embarrassed to admit that I actually thought I'd stepped through a time warp back to the 1800s—like in a *Twilight Zone* episode. I was so excited! My time-traveling experience deepened as I walked within earshot of the men. I could hear them talking to each other about who had died in the previous day's fighting and about the coming battle that day. When I cautiously approached, they promptly stood up and said, "Howdy, ma'am," and proceeded to tell me that fine ladies—one soldier actually called me a "fine lady"—shouldn't be anywhere near a battlefield.

I'd never heard of a Civil War reenactment before, so I was totally bewildered until one man "broke character" and took me aside to tell me that they were only pretending to be in the Civil War. (I felt completely foolish for thinking I'd entered into another time dimension.) He said that even though they were acting, it felt very real to them. I asked if they believed in reincarnation and he replied, using the Civil War dialect, "Yes, ma'am, some of the boys do believe they lived before, and they feel that they're reliving their past lives."

A historical event or time period that you feel strongly drawn to is most likely an indication of a past life, so it's valuable to examine this interest. My father didn't believe in reincarnation; however, he wasn't so sure after he explored our Scottish roots and ancestry. He told me about his experience standing on a high moor and suddenly "seeing" a battle and feeling that he absolutely knew every nuance of it as it unfolded before his eyes. This event was startling to him, and my dad felt as if he'd been there long ago.

Music

A song or musical score has the ability to transport us back to the time when we first heard it. A forgotten memory can be conjured simply by listening to a piece that was being played during the event. Just as music can help us evoke memories from this life, it can also spur remembrances of past lives.

Matt used to always hum the fiddle song "Turkey in the Straw" to himself. He never knew where he'd heard it, where it was from, or why he even liked it until he was at a gold-rush museum and realized that the same song was playing in the background. As he listened, he had spontaneous—and emotional—memories of panning for gold during the California gold rush in the mid-1800s.

Carly was visiting New Zealand when she heard the music of the native Maori people. She said that tears streamed down her face because the songs evoked such powerful emotions in her. She later participated in a past-life regression and remembered being a member of a Maori tribe.

Scents, Aromas, and Smells

Although we ascribe great importance to the way something looks or sounds, the way in which it smells can have an even more powerful effect on our emotions than any of our other senses. Research has shown that when we first meet someone, we'll like or dislike the person based more on the way he or she smells than on the way they look or sound . . . *even though we're not consciously aware of that individual's odor!*

A scent can instantly transport you to another time in history. Sally used to have a strong positive emotional response every time she smelled campfires despite the fact that her family had never gone camping—and she didn't ever remember being around a campfire as a child. It was only when she regressed and witnessed her previous life as a Native American in the area that's now Mexico that she realized where her profound love of the smell of campfires came from.

Kyle always felt at home whenever he picked up the scent of pine forests. He said that the aroma made him feel safe; and during a regression, he recalled a wonderful lifetime in Norway where he lived in a rich pine forest.

Although most people like the smell of meat cooking over an open fire, Hans hated it with a passion. When he discovered his difficult past life where he was in charge of human cremations that were conducted upon outdoor fires, he finally understood his strong distaste for the odor.

Déjà Vu Experiences

If you've ever been to a place for the first time yet felt that you'd been there before, write down your recollections. Also note occasions when you've met someone but felt that you already knew him or her. Psychologists say that déjà vu occurs when the scene that you're observing becomes available to your conscious mind a split second before you're consciously aware of it. You sense that you've seen it or been there before because you have—a fraction of a second earlier. However, I've found a direct correlation between déjà vu and past lives and believe that these events are very important in exploring reincarnation. Be sure to carefully record all of your déjà vu experiences.

One of the most emotional déjà vu episodes that I've ever encountered occurred while I was in Japan in the beautiful town of Kamakura. Standing in this city, resplendent with ancient temples, it's hard to imagine that Tokyo is only a short train ride away. A deep sense of the past is evident in every crevice of the numerous shrines and religious buildings there. When I walked into the Engakuji Temple, which was built in 1282 and dedicated to the Rinzai sect of Zen Buddhism, the familiarity of having stood there before was overwhelming. I *knew* that I'd been there before. As soon as I entered the grounds, the transformation within me was palpable. It was like being at a very noisy, busy airport; and then suddenly there is no sound. The feeling of déjà vu was profound! Everything about me changed—the way I walked, my mannerisms, my breathing pattern, and even my eyesight . . . I was able to see better. It was as if a past incarnation had partially overlapped my present life.

Although the grounds and the temple seemed very familiar, I didn't get the feeling that I had once actually lived there; rather, I felt that I was a monk who was visiting from another temple. The aching longing that I sensed while I was there was akin to a deep homesickness, but for something I couldn't quite remember.

Talents and Abilities

Many of the abilities that come to you spontaneously and easily can be attributed to past lives. Perhaps child prodigies—such as Mozart, who was a virtuoso at the harpsichord from an early age—acquire their abilities from previous lives. Examining your natural talents might offer additional clues as to who you once were.

One Saturday morning my daughter, Meadow, announced that she wanted to go ice-skating. She'd been watching a skating competition on television the evening before and had been enthralled by the beauty and grace that the skaters displayed. My husband, David, is usually very slow to move in the morning, so I was astounded when he immediately agreed to her request— especially since he'd never skated in his life.

Our experience at the rink surprised me. My daughter had roller-skated before but had never ice-skated, and quickly her ankles began to wobble as she plopped down onto the ice. I'd skated a lot as a child, but I was rusty and shaky. While I helped Meadow, we looked for David, the nonskater. Just at that moment, he sailed past us with the most smooth, graceful movements. He glided around us in circles. He skated backward. He skated fast and slow. He completed wondrous spins and turns. Astonishing!

After several minutes of pirouetting around the rink, David's feet suddenly flew out from under him and he pulled a muscle in his knee. It was as though something inside him knew exactly how to skate, but his muscles weren't prepared to move in those directions. Previously he'd recalled a life as a city official in Holland, and he had often skated on frozen canals and ponds. I believe that those distant memories of Holland had filtered through from his past.

Occupations and Hobbies

The occupations we're drawn to are usually the same as, or have similar features to, the ones we undertook in past lives. This seems to be especially true of vocations in early life. For example, one man whom I regressed had been a piano maker in Germany. In his current life, he learned to play that instrument as he was growing up, and in his 20s he became a carpenter. Both of these skills were connected to his previous life. Now he is neither a pianist nor a carpenter—he's an artist. I believe that he'd completed the karma from his prior German life, so he's no longer involved in the same occupations or hobbies.

Heritage and Ancestry

There's often a correlation between a person's cultural and/or racial heritage and the types of past lives he or she has experienced. This link isn't always evident, and to date there's been very little research into this phenomenon. You may find that you've shared a life with one or more of your ancestors. For instance, a man—whose great-grandfather had come from Spain—discovered that he was a woman in that incarnation and was married to his great-grandfather in that lifetime.

Sometimes you may even find that you *actually have been one of your own ancestors.* Deborah was surprised when, during a regression, she realized that she'd been her great-aunt Esther. Upon further research, she was even more astounded to discover an incredible number of similarities in their lives. For example, each year on her birthday, Deborah always performed a secret ceremony early in the morning. One by one, she'd remove 12 stones out of a small purse that she kept for the occasion (a stone for each month of the coming year) and as she did this she'd say out loud, "January is great! February is great!" and so on. Later in her life, Deborah was given Esther's diary and read her great-aunt's entries that recounted doing *the exact same thing!*

It's also common to have a number of past lives in the same heritage. So if you're of Scottish ancestry, you might have had a number of Scottish lifetimes; if you're of African descent, you might have had a number of African lifetimes. (I'm not sure if we actually have more lives in a particular heritage or if they're just easier to "remember" because they're somehow familiar to us.)

If others constantly assume that you're a different heritage than what you think you are, this can also be a past-life clue. For example, people continually asked Sandra if her family members had descended from Turkey, which she found strange since her ancestors were mostly from Belgium. Eventually this made sense when in a regression she uncovered a past life in Turkey.

Your Name

The name that you currently possess isn't an accident. In addition to providing you with the vibration and energy that you need for your current life, there are often past-life correlations with it. Explore possible past-life roots for your name by researching its origin and meaning. From what country does your name originate?

Dominique always wondered why his mother—whose parents were from Guatemala—gave him a French name. All of his brothers and sisters had Hispanic names except for him. However, when he discovered a lifetime in a French monastery and *his name was also Dominique,* he understood why he'd been given that name.

Sometimes the meaning of a name is a past-life clue. Devin read that his name was a Gaelic word for "poet" or "bard." He found this very interesting because in past-life regressions, he discovered numerous lifetimes in which he'd been a poet.

In addition, pay particular attention if your name was suddenly changed or came as a surprise to your parents at the time of your birth. For example, Jacob's mother and father had planned to call him Roger. But when his mother—who had just given birth to him moments before—was asked the name of her newborn son, she shocked herself by replying without hesitation, "His name is Jacob."

As an adult, Jacob experienced an incarnation in which he'd been an active member of the Jacobite rebellion in the British Isles during the 1700s. His fervent affiliation with the uprising created a powerful alignment with the name *Jacob.*

If you've been named after a family member, there's almost always a karmic connection with that individual. Rose had been named after her great-grandmother. Although she'd never met her, when she researched their family tree, she found remarkable similarities between the two of them. The similarities were so strong that the younger Rose became convinced that she'd been her great-grandmother in her former life.

John-George was named after his dad, and even though their relationship was always strained and competitive, the son discovered a significant past life. They'd experienced an earlier life together in Crete as brothers who were very competitive with each other.

Be sure not to overlook the nicknames that either you take on yourself or that others give you. A woman named Merry was called "Medici" for her entire life, for no obvious reason that anyone could remember. However, during a regression she uncovered a life in Italy as part of the powerful Medici family.

Books and Films

Searching for clues to your past lives can be as easy as reading travel guides, watching films situated in other countries or time periods, or flipping through *National Geographic* magazines to observe your reactions to various scenes and images. Read about different cultures in an encyclopedia (or online) and note which ones you find most interesting. Look at picture books of various environments and notice how they affect you. For example, check out some photographs of desert settings and see if you experience any emotional reactions to them. If you do feel a response, use your imagination to put yourself in the picture, and imagine what you might have looked like or what kind of life you'd be leading if you were really there.

What types of books have you been attracted to throughout your life? As a child, I read everything that I could find about the Amazon. Those steamy jungle scenes—and especially stories about anacondas—fascinated me. I also loved going to the zoo to look at these creatures up close and persuaded my parents to introduce me to a snake expert. Holding an anaconda was one of the thrills of my childhood, and eventually I even raised and bred snakes. But there was nothing in my upbringing that foreshadowed this passion of mine; however, in my past-life exploration, I uncovered a life as an early Spanish explorer in which I was spellbound by the incredible wildlife and natural wonders of this mighty river.

Examining the types of books, movies, and magazines that you're drawn to is valuable as you research past lives. Jot down a list of the images and scenes from your favorite novels and films that have particularly impressed you. In addition, pay attention to specific themes that are enthralling or appeal to you—or even repel you. For instance, I can't watch scenes where someone is treated unfairly. I can account for this because I've experienced unjust treatment in my life, and I've also traced it back to previous lifetimes.

Animals and Pets

Do you feel a kinship with certain kinds of animals? When you're around these beings, do you feel that you're able to communicate with them? This type of experience may be related to a past life in which you had extensive contact with a particular kind of animal. Perhaps you were a horse trainer or a farmer. Or maybe at some point, your only friend was a pet. The emotional solace provided by that relationship might have been the one thing that kept you going through an incredibly difficult situation. There are accounts of prisoners who formed bonds with rats in their cells and even saved portions of their meager rations to feed their little friends. These acts of kindness, along with gratitude for the animals, kept these individuals from going insane.

To the ancient Egyptians, cats represented gods. Relics of that time are filled with regal pictures of cats acting out the civilization's most important myths. In fact, cats were so honored that many of them were embalmed along with their owners when they died. If you've had a lifelong affinity for cats, to the point of nearly worshipping them, you might have had a life in ancient Egypt.

Sometimes an animal that unreasonably frightens you can be an important sign. For example, Donald was terrified of alligators. He was so frightened that he refused to swim in his pool at night because of his intense fear—even though there were no alligators in New Mexico where he lived. Donald told me that although he knew that he truly wasn't in danger, he couldn't seem to overcome his irrational fear. It was only when he healed a past life—in which he'd been dragged into the water and mauled by a crocodile—that he could finally enjoy nighttime swims in his pool without fear.

Personality Traits, Mannerisms, and Habitual Behaviors

More details about your past lives can be found by studying the mannerisms, personality quirks, and behaviors that make you unique. Of course many of these characteristics can be traced to events and influences in your present life, but the traits that are completely out of keeping with your upbringing can be explained by exploring past lives. People often exhibit behavior that, on the surface, makes no sense in terms of their personal history. For example, a very mild-mannered man, who came from a gracious and kind family, noticed that whenever he witnessed cruelty to children, he felt sudden violent anger and often had to be restrained to prevent him from hurting someone. This man said that at times he'd even wanted to kill individuals just for yelling at their kids. He was shocked by his own behavior. However, he began to understand where this trait came from when he delved into his past lives.

In a previous incarnation, this man discovered that as a child he'd lived in an orphanage where children were abused. During that lifetime, he wished he could kill the cruel supervising officials. He balanced the distress of that situation by incarnating into a peaceful, loving family; however, he still carried the residue of abhorrence that had filtered into his current life regarding kids being ill-treated.

Carefully examine any unusual qualities that you may possess. For example, some people, despite having grown up in poverty, have refined mannerisms and behave as if they were royalty. Even as children, they loved luxurious things and acted as though they'd had them in spite of their destitute living conditions. It's likely that such individuals experienced lives of privilege in previous lifetimes.

Sometimes habitual behaviors can be explained in terms of reincarnation. Every night before going to sleep, Jeremy always had to look under the bed, to the chagrin of his long-patient wife. When he reexperienced a past life in China—in which an assassin had lain in waiting beneath his bed and then killed him—he realized why he was obsessed with checking under the bed every night.

Fran had a peculiar trait of bowing to everyone she met. Although this isn't unusual behavior for someone who had a previous life in Asia, it *was* considered strange in her present life.

Relationships

Perhaps more than any other clue, the dynamics of your relationships can offer powerful insights into who you were. We tend to subconsciously and symbolically re-create events from our far past, especially from those experiences that were never resolved. Every reenactment is a way to heal those unsettled situations. For example, when Moses and John were growing up, they were next-door neighbors. They were friends but Moses always tended to resent John, and for some reason John put up with it. One summer the two teens decided to go on a canoe trip together. As they paddled, their canoe overturned and Moses was caught in the current. John, at great effort—and almost at the expense of his own life—was able to rescue Moses.

From that point their relationship almost magically transformed, and Moses no longer resented his friend. John later discovered that in a past life, they'd both been native South Americans. On a canoe trip during that lifetime, Moses had fallen out of the boat but John didn't try to save him. Moses had drowned, which caused the lingering resentment in the present time. Reliving the original event shifted the dynamics between them. (Remember, it can be a symbolic or an actual reenactment of the situation. For example, if Moses felt that he was *drowning* financially and John had saved him, that also might have balanced the original karma.)

Often the way you *feel* about someone is a reflection of a past connection. For instance, whenever Jill talked about her friend Sandy, she called her "my sister." And if Sandy had a problem, Jill used to say—without knowing why—"Hey, Sandy, I'm your older sister; I'll take care of it for you!"

Jill discovered that in a previous life, Sandy *had* been her younger sister. This explained why she felt the need to protect and support Sandy in her current life.

When you instantly like someone, or immediately dislike the individual, this is usually because of a past-life connection. Sometimes roles will reverse, creating new challenges. In a past incarnation, Ron was the father of his current dad. So in his present-day life, he resented his dad telling him what to do. Subconsciously he thought, *Hey, wait a minute! I'm the father; I should be the one passing out orders here.*

Also, just because someone seems to be your enemy in this life, it doesn't necessarily mean that there's a negative past life. In some cases, a very loving soul mate will incarnate *at your request* to be your worthy opponent; as a result, *you* are able to gain strength, clarity, and wisdom as you overcome your adversary. In other words, this individual came in order to help you grow. By carefully examining all your relationships, and especially the recurring patterns, you can begin to understand the dynamics of your past.

Causes You're Passionate About

Think about the causes you've contributed to over the years—whether financially or with your time and energy. Usually there's a connection between a past life and a movement or principle that's truly meaningful to you. Devi was a devout advocate of saving old-growth forests. At one point, she'd even considered tying herself to a tree to protest the destruction of an ancient forest. She traced this activism to a peaceful and wonderful past life in which she'd lived alone in the Bavarian woods. During that time, she loved trees and used to talk to them; they were her friends. So in this life, she took it upon herself to try to help her friends.

Another woman, who had been tortured because of her political beliefs in a past life, is a strong supporter of Amnesty International in her current life and passionately fights to end the inhumane treatment of political prisoners.

Traumatic Events

As I mentioned earlier, the distressing events in your life are usually symbolic reenactments of past-life traumas that haven't healed. Again it's important to remember the following: *It isn't the actual ordeal creating a blockage that's carried forward into your current life; it's the limiting decisions and judgments that you made at the time of the incident that carry forward.* For example, let's say that two women each lost a child in a previous life. One woman had decided that she never wants to become pregnant again because she's afraid that she might lose another child, but the second woman had chosen instead to cherish every relationship because she'll never know how long it will last.

The devastating events are identical, but how each person reacted at the time is very different. The first woman, in her current life, might notice that she's afraid to get close to anyone or she may have trouble getting pregnant; and the second woman might notice that she passionately embraces every single one of her relationships. It's the same situation but with two different meanings.

Fears and Phobias

Many people can't explain the fears and phobias they have, even after years of traditional therapy. Sometimes it's only by working through traumas experienced during past lives that these problems can be unraveled. For example, a middle-aged woman had an extreme fear of snakes, which prevented her from doing the things she'd otherwise very much enjoy. She was extremely afraid to walk anywhere outside, even in relatively safe areas, for fear of coming into contact with a snake. Nightmares about these reptiles kept her awake for weeks at a time. Finally, through past-life regression, she discovered that she was once lowered into a snake pit as punishment for a petty crime she'd committed in an ancient and barbarous culture she'd lived in. The subconscious fear that this could happen to her again for some small thing that she might unwittingly do haunted her for years, until she became aware of the original source of her terror and healed it.

Examination of our most persistent fears and phobias, especially those that seem unrelated to our present existence, can be a useful tool for deciphering clues to earlier incarnations. Many people choose to do past-life work because frightening experiences in previous lives often recur in the present. You'll find that whatever you fear will return again and again until you overcome it— this is a cosmic law. So examine what makes you afraid. You could even imagine possible past-life scenarios to accompany your phobias in order to gain further insight about who you were.

Words and Phrases You Use

As you uncover who you were, it's valuable to begin to carefully listen to the phrases that you use regularly and to specific words that you employ to describe something or someone. Arnold was upset with a co-worker, and he repeatedly told me that he felt like he'd been "stabbed in the back" by this person. During a past-life regression, he relived an experience in Macedonia in which his present-day colleague had indeed stabbed him in the back.

Another man always used the expression "jumping through hoops." For example, he'd say, "Boy, my boss sure had me jumping through hoops today!" Or if the roadways were hectic during his commute, he'd remark, "That traffic jam had me jumping though hoops." It turned out that in his past life as a gypsy, he developed a special kind of dance in which he *jumped through hoops*.

Bud used to repeatedly say, "Let's call in the troops!" or "The troops have arrived!" or "Don't let the troops down!" When he uncovered a past life in the United States cavalry of the old West, he understood why he used that expression.

Danielle would always complain, "That drives me crazy!" She probably said it 50 times a day. In her regression, she discovered a previous life spent in the area that's now Estonia; and during that time, she suffered from severe mental problems.

Sometimes we're not aware of the expressions we say because we blurt them out unconsciously. Consider asking some friends whether they've noticed if you've continually used certain phrases or words.

Body Type

Although we have different body types in our various lives, sometimes there are aspects that carry over from a previous lifetime. Usually this only occurs if there's a blockage or emotional response that wasn't cleared from an earlier life, but sometimes it happens because we strongly identify with a characteristic.

Ronald was born with one arm slightly deformed. Because of it, he always thought that he was beneath others and convinced himself that people didn't respect him. Surprisingly, when I asked him how it made him feel, he said that he felt like a coward. When I regressed him back in time, he relived a life as a Japanese warrior. He had seriously injured his arm (not in battle) and consequently wasn't allowed to fight. Being disposed of by his commanders made him feel inferior and even weak for not fighting alongside his compatriots. Healing that lifetime didn't change the status of his arm, but he no longer felt subservient nor did he view himself as a coward.

Sometimes body types can reverse throughout lifetimes as a kind of karmic balance. For instance, Helen had a past life as a large, overbearing man who considered himself superior to others because of his size and shape. But in her current life, Helen is very petite and constantly experiences people looming over her. Remember, this body-type reversal isn't a punishment; it just allows us to develop compassion and understanding for others.

Health Issues

Oftentimes, health challenges carry forward from earlier lives. An incident that's similar to a previous-life event can activate an unaccounted pain or injury that originated in the far past. For example, in Amy's past life she was banished from her tribe for adulterous activity. (She was a man in that lifetime.) She was so distraught that she threw herself off a cliff and died from a head injury. In her present life, every time that she'd had a single thought of having an affair, she was overcome with a debilitating migraine headache. She had subconsciously equated adultery with dying of a head injury; so in her present life, even the thought of an affair would activate severe pain in her head.

Additionally, a disease or illness that you had at a particular age in your past life can emerge at the same age in your present life. This will only happen if there are unresolved emotional issues that accompanied this event. Dakota developed a terrible rash that covered her body when she was 25 years old. The onset was sudden and dramatic and even erupted into severe blisters. In a regression, she *saw* a past life in which she'd been 25 years old and had been burned at the stake for being a witch.

There can also be residual memories of health issues that will filter into the present and manifest in your current body. Heart problems (or a broken heart) in a past life can resurface as heart disease in a current life. Body-weight insecurities in an earlier incarnation could recur in a present life. However, health problems will only be repeated if there were unresolved issues of this kind during the past-life experience.

Some present-day health concerns are a symbolic manifestation of a past-life trauma. For example, throat problems can come from an incarnation in which you were hanged, strangled, or killed for speaking your truth. Chest pain may arise from drowning, suffocating, or being crushed. Severe headaches could be due to massive head wounds or battle injuries; and even stomach illnesses could result from poisoning, malnutrition, starving, or being stabbed in the gut.

Scars, Birthmarks, and Tattoos

There's a definite correlation between scars, birthmarks, and tattoos that you may have in this life and what has occurred in your past lives. In a regression, a woman vividly remembered having been shot in the forehead in another life. Interestingly enough, this woman found an unusual, small indentation beneath her hairline that looked as if a small bullet had penetrated there. Another woman realized that a scar she'd had from an appendix operation was in the exact same place as a sword wound she'd received in a battle in ancient Persia.

Even birthmarks can carry clues to past lives. I suggest that you examine your birthmarks and ask yourself what might have made those specific kinds of marks; then pay attention to any images or feelings that well up from within you. (Your emotional responses often contain clues to your past lives.) For example, George had a birthmark that looked as if half of his face had been badly burned. He visited a previous life and discovered that he'd righteously punished others by scalding them with hot oil as penance for crimes they'd committed. (Once again, please note that his birthmark was *not* karmic retribution from an avenging god; instead, it was a way that George's spirit had chosen to develop more compassion for himself and others.)

Tattoos can also give past-life hints. Over a number of years, Marie had had Celtic symbols tattooed on various parts of her body and was comforted when she discovered a previous life in Ireland as a blacksmith. Ted experienced similar feelings regarding a powerful past life in China that correlated with the Chinese characters that he'd tattooed on his body.

Injuries, Diseases, and Surgeries

Not only are the injuries and diseases that you've endured often indicative of past-life experiences, but the emotions that have accompanied them are also very telling. Sue-Ann used to become unusually despondent and even fatalistic every time she caught a cold. She'd think of her life as if it were over and would dwell on her seemingly impending death. She couldn't figure out why even the most nonthreatening illnesses would invite these feelings—until she experienced a past life in Portugal in which a summer cold had quickly led to pneumonia and then to her death.

Repeat accidents are almost always an indication of an unresolved past-life trauma. As a child, Jonathan fell in his family's barn and one of the prongs of a pitchfork pierced his right thigh. As an adult, he was doing some work outside and fell off a ladder; and the iron stake in his fence punctured his right thigh in *exactly the same place.* In a past-life regression, he relived an event where, as an Australian aborigine, he'd been speared through his right thigh as punishment for breaking a taboo.

To delve even deeper into your previous lives, whenever you're hurt, imagine that you're actually becoming very tiny and traveling into the injury or wound. Then allow images and memories to rise to the surface. The closer to the time of the injury, the easier it is to discover your incarnation.

Dreams

A powerful way to gain understanding of past lives without experiencing a regression is by examining your dreams. Later in this book, I'll discuss their significance and provide more information about reincarnation. Many dreams contain secret messages regarding not only your current life and relationships, but also those in your far past . . . and even in your future lives.

Additional (Nonregression) Techniques

Although the most powerful past-life experiences are usually revealed through regressions, here are some alternative methods that you can use to gain clues about who you've been.

Look in a Mirror

Become very still and relaxed. In a dimly lit room (candlelight is best), stare at your reflection in a mirror. Sometimes your face will change shape, and you can begin to see how you might have looked in a previous incarnation. Periodically close your eyes and note if any images arise spontaneously. *Relax.* Open your mind to the infinity of the universe and the endless possibilities in your own past.

If you begin to feel unsure or disoriented, take a break and try again later. As a suggestion, keep a notepad next to you and record any impressions that you have—no matter how fleeting they might be. You also might want to try a variation of this technique, which is described next.

One-on-One

This is similar to the mirror technique except that you do it with a friend who's seated across from you. When you practice this method, it's important to choose someone whom you trust deeply and can help you process whatever feelings may arise.

Working with a partner can be done in one of two ways. You can look into each other's face and mutually search for clues as to whom the other person was in another life. (As a suggestion, just stare intently into one eye rather than shifting your focus back and forth.) Or you could take turns: Examine your partner's face first, as he or she simply sits still and relaxes. In either case, you'll be concentrating in the same way as you would if you were doing the mirror exercise. You'll often start to see the other person's face change, and the individual will seem to look different. Sometimes your partner may appear as the opposite gender or even a different race or age. Trust your intuition as you pick up past-life clues. And again, it's valuable to record your impressions while they're still fresh.

Chapter Five

Past-Life Clues Questionnaire

The following questionnaire will help you open the door into your previous incarnations; in addition, it's specifically designed as a kind of touchstone to activate memories, emotions, and images from long ago. In almost mystical ways, each question acts as a key to unlock your past.

Go through this chapter in a thoughtful manner. Proceed slowly, allowing yourself to reflect, breathe, and contemplate. Ask yourself, *If the answer to this question opened a portal to another time period, where would I be . . . and who would I have been?* The more time and energy you allow, the more likely you are to truly discover who you were.

Notice the feelings that each question elicits. As you embark on this comprehensive journey, stay in touch with any emotions or spontaneous physical sensations that begin to emerge while writing down your answers. You'll gain clearer and more accurate insights the more thorough you are in accessing your responses.

As a suggestion, center yourself before each question. If a seemingly unrelated thought or memory arises as you do the exercise, write it down in what I call your *Past-Life Detective Journal.* Pay attention to *all* of your reactions; sometimes a small clue can open a big door.

Childhood Games

As a child, you didn't have the strong filters most adults later develop that block out past-life memories; therefore, careful examination of games you enjoyed when you were little can often reveal significant evidence about who you were.

- What were the types of games you played as a child? List them. Were any of these unusual for someone of your age?

- As you go through your list, were there any activities that consistently brought up particular emotions?

- When you were playing make-believe, what did you envision?

- Did your friends play any games that made you feel uncomfortable?

- What did you like to wear for Halloween or costume parties?

Childhood Preferences and Inclinations

The consistent attitudes and preferences you exhibited in your youth can be very telling in regard to events from a past existence. List every single idiosyncrasy that was unique to you as a child. Then think about what kind of previous life might have been responsible for that personal inclination.

- What consistent attitudes did you have about life as a youth? For example, were you exhilarated, pessimistic, optimistic, or patient?

- Did you have any habits or predilections that were uncommon for a child of your age?

- Did your family members tell you about anything unusual you did?

- Were you more inclined to want to be: inside or outside, with people or alone, busy or idle, talking or quiet, sleeping by yourself or with others?

- When given choices, did you have any strong preferences?

Clothing Styles

As you examine your clothing preferences, be aware of any styles that you're drawn to from particular cultures or time periods. Also think about the kinds of outfits you like to wear to costume parties.

- What styles of clothing do you really like and dislike?

- What types make you feel comfortable (or very uncomfortable) when you wear them?

- What is your favorite outfit and why?

- Do you feel more at home in formal or casual wear? Are you most comfortable wearing military, free-flowing, or peasant-style outfits? Lace, flowers, or something else?

- Do you prefer a high neckline or a low one? Long or short skirts? Snug- or tight-fitting clothes?

- Which do you like more: hot- or cold-weather clothes?

- Would you rather wear cotton, wool, silk, linen, or synthetic fabrics? Have you ever made your own clothes or had outfits made for you? What style were these clothes?

- What foot coverings feel the most comfortable? Do you prefer boots, shoes, sandals, moccasins, bare feet, or something else? Be specific. If you chose boots, do you like cowboy boots, military-style, hiking, or some other kind?

- What style of jewelry do you find attractive? Do you like to wear a lot of it, just a small amount, or none at all? Are there any particular clothing accessories that you really enjoy?

- Go through your wardrobe . . . are there any styles that could fit into a particular time in history?

Architecture and Home-Furnishing Styles

Think about the types of architecture you find comforting or inspiring (or irritating or agitating). Take a moment to look around your home, and observe your surroundings objectively. Be aware of any furnishings from a particular era or geographical location. Are there rooms or areas of your home in which you feel very comfortable? Of course there could be many reasons for this feeling, but it may be that the items in that space are reminiscent of ones from past incarnations. Additionally, draw a picture of your perfect home—inside and out—and notice what emotions and images arise as you do so.

- What is your favorite architectural style? What is your least favorite?

- If you could live in any style of home from any time in history, what would you choose?

- What type of furniture do you like or strongly dislike?

- What are your favorite objects or accents in your home? Why? Do they represent a specific culture or historical period?

- What objects, artwork, or posters decorate your walls? What drew them to you?

- What do you have on the floor? Are there scatter rugs, Asian carpets, ethnic hand-loomed rugs, hardwood floors, or something else?

- What colors are predominant in your home?

- If money wasn't an object, in what style would you furnish your home?

- Have you moved around a lot in your life, or do you have a tendency to stay in one place?

Food Preferences and Eating Habits

List your favorite and least favorite types of food. Notice what emotions each food elicits in you. Stand in your kitchen and notice how you feel when you're in there or as you're preparing a meal.

- As a child, what foods did you love and hate? Was there any particular way that you used to enjoy eating your meals?

- How do you consume your food? Do you eat quickly, almost as if it were your last meal (like someone who normally doesn't have much to eat), or do you eat in an elegant and refined manner (like someone who has the luxury of picking at their food)?

- Do you like to eat a big meal early in the day (for example, someone who works long hours outdoors may need a hearty breakfast)? Do you prefer to start with a light breakfast and lunch and then have a large late-night meal (like many people in Mediterranean countries have done through time)?

- Do you ever notice any personality change in yourself when you eat different kinds of food? For example, when you eat Italian food, do you find yourself becoming more flamboyant? When you eat Japanese food, do you behave more demurely?

- When preparing meals, what do you tend to cook on a regular basis? Are there some foods that you don't like to prepare? Do you frequently use particular cooking utensils?

- Are there any foods that always upset your stomach? Are there any that bring on an emotional response within you—either positive or negative?

Allergies

Some allergies are lessened (and even cured) simply by discovering their past-life source. List any allergies that you currently have or have had in the past. Next to each one, jot down what was occurring in your life at the same time.

- What are you allergic to?

- Have you ever had a severe allergic reaction? What was happening at the same time in your life?

- Have you ever experienced an allergy that spontaneously disappeared? What was going on in your life then?

- What was occurring at the onset of the allergy?

- At the start of an allergic reaction, what emotion do you feel?

- If you were to imagine a past life in which someone experienced that same reaction *and* that particular emotion, what might that past life have been?

Geographical Locations

Geographical preferences can be a potent past-life indicator. Write down locations that evoke an emotional response within you whether it's positive or negative.

- What countries have you always wanted to visit? Where have you *never* wanted to go?

- If you could vacation anywhere in the world, where would you go and why?

- What kind of terrain makes you feel at your best—and where do you feel the worst? Is it at the desert, plains, mountains, rain forest, pine forest, beach, lake, or woods? Is it in a meadow, savanna, or by rolling hills, valleys, or canyons?

- Which do you prefer: cities, towns, villages, farms, ranches, or the countryside?

Climates

If you love extreme, arid heat, perhaps you once lived in a desert; or if you prefer the clean, crisp coolness of wintertime, you may have enjoyed a past life in a land of snow and ice. Imagine yourself in different climates and note the emotional responses you have to each.

- What's your favorite type of climate? What kind of weather makes you feel happy? Sad? Depressed? Content? Creative?

- Do you prefer being outside or indoors? What sort of activities do you associate with different climates?

- What countries have the kind of climate that you like (and dislike) the most? (Although many countries have similar climates, the first names that pop into your mind may be a clue.)

- If finances weren't an issue, in what type of climate would you live year-round?

Cultures

There's often a correlation between the cultures that fascinate you and your past incarnations. For example, someone who's deeply interested in Native Americans, ancient Egypt, or the Aztec civilization may find that he or she has experienced a previous life in that society. Also notice the ethnic designs that appeal or feel familiar to you. Look at symbols from various peoples such as Celtic, Egyptian, Maori, Native American, African, Chinese, Japanese, East Indian, Viking, Roman, and Middle Eastern.

- As a child, were there particular cultures that interested you? Did you ever focus on a certain one for a school project? Were there books about this subject that you enjoyed reading as a youngster?

- As an adult, have you ever studied or developed a deep curiosity about a specific culture?

- Did you ever spend time in a different culture that felt like home?

- If you could choose to live in any culture, which one would you select?

Time Periods or Historical Events

Examine periods in history that have interested you in your present life. Cast your mind back to your school days—was there a particular era that appealed to you then, such as the Stone Age, the Bronze Age, the ancient rule of the pharaohs, the Middle Ages, the Renaissance, or the Industrial Revolution? Are there historical events that captivate you now? Perhaps you're intrigued by the French Revolution, American Revolution, World War I, or the Vikings' discovery of the New World?

Briefly consult any world-history reference work to see if there's a certain epoch that stands out in your mind; however, remember that many books of this genre ignore native cultures, so you'll have to look in anthropology books for this type of information.

- If you could magically transport yourself back to a specific period in history, when would it be? Why?

- If you were paid a great deal of money to research a historical event of your choosing, what would it be? Why?

- If you could be a famous person in history, whom would you pick? Why?

- What event in history would you want to learn the whole, unbiased truth about?

Music

When you listen to music, is there a certain kind that creates images in your mind? Imagine that you're traveling the world and hearing the rhythms and songs from every country and time period. Is there a particular era or area that you really like or dislike?

- As a child, was there a specific kind of music that you liked or disliked?

- What's your favorite type of music now?

- Is there a genre that always makes you happy (or sad)? What kinds make you feel emotional?

- Have you ever learned to play a musical instrument? Do you still play it? Were you able to learn it easily—that is, did it seem familiar to you?

- Is there a particular instrument that ignites an emotional response within you, such as the sound of a drumbeat, violin, or gamelan?

- Have you ever taken singing lessons? When you're singing to yourself, is there a particular kind of song you like to perform?

- Have you ever had a song repeat itself over and over in your head? What was it? Were there images or memories associated with it?

- When you hear people singing, is there a particular type of music that you respond to? Choral arrangements? Gregorian or Tibetan overtone chanting?

Scents, Aromas, and Smells

Almost all smells have subconscious memories associated with them. Notice the powerful reactions—positive and negative—that you've had to certain odors you've encountered in your life. Then imagine what kind of experience someone might have had in order to strongly like or dislike that particular scent.

You might consider testing a series of essential oils (samples are usually available at health-food stores) to find out which ones appeal to you and which ones don't. This exercise can also help open the door to the past. If you respond to a certain scent, inhale it and imagine that this aroma is carrying you back to another era (and be sure to notice where you've arrived).

- As a child, do you remember any smells that you strongly liked or disliked?

- Imagine gently breathing in each of the following aromas and see if any spontaneous memories arise (after each one, I've listed where it was popular in past times): frankincense or myrrh, Middle East; sandalwood, India; eucalyptus, Australia; lemon, Italy; juniper, Tibet; lavender, France; sage, North America; and rose, England.

- What scents do you love or hate? Have you ever had an immediate and powerful emotional reaction to an odor but didn't know why?

- What scents from nature do you love? Which human-made smells do you have strong emotional responses to?

Déjà Vu Experiences

If you've ever had a profound déjà vu experience, go back in your mind to that event and relive it as fully as you can. Allow any associated feelings, images, or impressions to emerge as you do so. Write down everything that you remember.

- Have you ever experienced déjà vu? Where were you and what was your emotional response to it each time?

- If you were asked to create a drama that included the particular place where the déjà vu occurred, what would you write?

Talents and Abilities

Talents from our past lives will often emerge during our childhood years . . . and then sometimes they'll recede as we enter adulthood. Think about any unusual talents you possessed as a child or whether you feel a natural pull toward any particular skills. List these abilities and imagine that if there was a past life associated with each one of these talents, what would that life have been like?

- If other people described your raw talents, what would they say? What do you consider your inherent abilities to be? In what particular area of your life do you naturally excel?

- Has there been a time when you surprised yourself by innately knowing how to do something? What was it?

- Have you ever immersed yourself so thoroughly in the creation of something that time seemed to disappear?

- Are there some talents that you possess that you take for granted that others find difficult?

- What abilities do you admire in others? Which ones do you dislike?

- Is there something that you do extremely well but really don't enjoy doing it?

- Have you ever created something—or truly excelled at something—that evoked strong and familiar emotions?

Occupations and Hobbies

Your career can give you important clues into your far past and can often indicate skills that you possessed in one or more of your previous incarnations. Sometimes your occupation is a continuing aspect of an earlier one; or as a way to balance karma, your current job could be a *reversal* of those that you had in past lives.

- When you were a child, what did you want to be when you grew up? Did you follow your childhood passion? Were there aspects of your youthful desires that you pursued?

- What is your present career? Do you like it? Is it easy or difficult for you?

- What are the primary reasons why you work? Is it for the money, creativity, social activity, benefits, or the workplace environment?

- If money wasn't an object, what would your occupation be? How would you spend your time? What would you want to achieve or accomplish?

- Do you feel that you're doing what you're meant to be doing? Or do you have a longing to be doing something else—even if you don't know what that is?

- Did you search for your current job, or did it seemingly fall into your lap? Is it something that you would have chosen for yourself?

- Have you ever been self-employed? Was it a good match for you, or are you more comfortable working for someone else?

- Is there any aspect of your career that feels familiar or that elicits strong emotions?

- Do you have any hobbies? If your hobby involves directions, do you need to follow them or do you easily complete your project without guidance?

- Do you collect things? What and why do you collect them? What feelings do they activate within you?

- If you could pursue any hobby, without money or time as a consideration, what would you enjoy doing? Why?

Heritage and Ancestry

If you don't know much about your ancestry, as a suggestion, you may want to do some research to become more familiar with your roots. Many people find that this dovetails very well with their own past-life exploration.

- What is your heritage? Do you identify more closely with the ancestry of your mother or of your father?

- Do you feel attracted to any cultures that are also a part of your heritage?

- Are you closely aligned with any of your ancestors, or are there any whom you identify with?

- Do you strongly dislike or are you ashamed of any of your ancestors?

- What lineage is your family name from?

- Are there any battles or historical events in alignment with your heritage that are especially meaningful to you?

- Do other people always assume that you're of a different heritage than you actually are?

Your Name

Your birth name holds the vibration and energy of who you are in your current life; however, it can also provide valuable insights into your previous lives. Research the origins of your name, and talk to family members.

- When you were growing up, did you have any nicknames? Did you have any names that you insisted people call you instead of your birth-given name?

- What's the meaning of your birth-certificate name?

- Did your parents have a name picked out that they suddenly changed right before (or after) you were born?

- What nationality is your name? Is it the same nationality as your parents' names?

- What's the meaning of your name? Do you have a name that you go by that isn't your legal name? What's the significance of that

name, and what does it mean to you?
How did it come to you?

- Are you named after someone—a family
  member, perhaps? Do you know him or
  her? What do you know about that person?
  Do you like or admire this individual?

Books and Films

Make a list of times when you've read a book or
watched a movie and felt instantly transported into a
realm that seemed real and *familiar* to you. In addition,
write down any intensely strong emotions that surprised
you while you were reading or watching a movie. Your
lists are good starting points for past-life exploration.

- What is your favorite book? Why?

- Is there a particular historical period or
  event that you love to read about?

- As a child, was there a particular book that
  fascinated you or one that you read over
  and over? What was it about the story that
  made such an impression on you?

- Have you ever written a fictional story?
  What was it about, and when did it occur?
  What kind of stories do you like to read?

- Is there any particular kind of poetry that tugs at your heart? Do you prefer reading haiku or sonnets? Do you have a favorite writer, such as Rumi, Emerson, or Shakespeare?

- Are there any specialty magazines you subscribe to? Why?

- Is there a particular character from a book or film whom you profoundly identified with or vehemently disliked?

- What types of movies or TV series do you like or dislike? Westerns? War movies? Shows about families? Action films? Medical dramas? Historical epics? Cop shows? Love stories?

- Are there any types of shows that activate strong emotions in you?

Animals and Pets

Carefully analyzing the types of animals you're drawn to—as well as those you're afraid of—can offer remarkable clues to your past. Make a list of all the animals you've been attached to, fascinated with, or terrified of in your life. After each entry, imagine a past-life scenario that includes the animal and your associated emotions. Write it all down.

- What animals do you love or admire? Which ones do you dislike?

- If you were an animal, what kind do you think others would associate with you?

- If you had to be an animal, which kind would you *like* to be?

- Do you have any paintings, statues, or figurines of a certain animal in your home?

- Do you have collections of one particular kind of animal? Why? What associations do you have with that species?

- Have you discovered your totem animal? What is it? In what part of the world or historical time period were these animals revered?

Personality Traits, Mannerisms, and Habitual Behaviors

Your personality wasn't just formed upon birth; it's the outcome of a long line of incarnations. It's also not uncommon, as a karmic balancing, to undergo a complete personality reversal. For example, an individual could be overly strong willed in one life and then unassertive and timid in the following one—however, they're two sides of the same coin. Jot down the adjectives that best describe you. Look at this list and imagine that someone in history had these same qualities; think about where this person might have lived and what might have been their occupation.

- How would others describe your personality? How would you describe it? Do you have any personality quirks?

- What's your most usual disposition—that is, what emotions do you experience the most often, on a consistent basis? Write these down. Use your imagination to visualize what kind of person in history might have experienced these exact same emotions regularly.

- Do you have any unusual mannerisms or routines? Do you talk with an accent but have no way to account for it?

- Do you have any habitual behaviors but aren't quite sure why or how they started? List them. If a historical play were performed that starred someone who exhibited these same characteristics, who and what might that person be?

Relationships

Every one of your important relationships is with someone you've known before. Additionally, the patterns that occur with partners in your current life have their source in your past. Make a list of every significant relationship that you've had in your life—ones that you deemed both positive and negative. Then after each entry, write a few words that describe the relationship's dynamics and how it feels or felt at the time. For example, you might write "feels like fellow warriors," "feels like sister and brother," or "feels like mother and son." Notice any past-life images that begin to emerge as you do this exercise.

- As a child, who was most important to you? Whom did you feel safe with? Was there anyone you felt unsafe around? Who loved you and whom did you love?

- When your parents commanded you to do something, did you happily obey or feel that they didn't have the right to order you around?

- What was the main way that you related to people as a child? Were you shy or aloof, or did you want to be the life of the party? Did you desire to be lord of the manor? Were you always trying to make everyone happy?

- As an adult, what patterns—regarding your relationships—seem to recur? Do you constantly attend to the needs of others, even to the detriment of your needs? Do you sabotage relationships? Are you often betrayed by others, or do you betray people? Are you taken advantage of frequently, or do you take advantage of others?

- Who have been your best friends? When you met them, did you feel an instant bond? Who have been your enemies? When you first came into contact with these individuals, did you immediately have feelings of like or dislike toward them?

- Do you feel close to your family, or have you felt that you've never quite belonged? *Whom* do you feel most connected to—both in a negative and positive way—and which family member do you feel the most detached from?

Causes You're Passionate About

Oftentimes, there's a direct correlation between the causes you're passionate about and your far past, especially if your beliefs stir deep emotions within you.

- Make a list of all the causes you've contributed your time, energy, or money to.

- Even if you've never donated money to a charity or nonprofit organization, which causes do you believe in fervently?

- If you were given $10,000 that had to be given away to a worthy cause, which would you choose and why?

- Is there a movement or organization that you strongly disagree with? Why?

- If you were going to start a charity or you had the opportunity to create or build something that would benefit humanity, what would it be and why?

Traumatic Events

Almost every traumatic experience has its source in a past life. List every distressing event you can remember, and after each one, write your emotional response to it.

- What's the worst thing you've ever experienced? What did you learn from it?

- If you felt frightened during a trauma, try to think of other times in your life when you endured a similar kind of fear. Write them down.

- If you could give different and positive meanings to each of the traumatic episodes in your life, what would they be?

- If soul dramas, set in different time periods, were created around each of these upsetting events, what might each one entail?

- Is your life fairly even in nature, or do you experience extreme highs and lows?

Fears and Phobias

When exploring your fears and phobias, pay particular attention to those that seemingly have no roots in your current life. Simply imagining a past-life scenario to accompany that fear or phobia can often unlock the key to an unresolved trauma that has been carried forward into the present.

- What is your greatest fear? What terrifies you to even think of it? If someone in another lifetime had that exact fear, what kind of past life might explain it?

- When you're frightened, is there any other emotion that often accompanies that fear?

- What types of situations scare you the most? Is there a recurring theme?

- What do you think is the most terrifying thing that could happen to someone else?

- Do you have any seemingly unreasonable phobias? What sort of past-life experiences might account for this? Use your imagination to explore this idea.

Words and Phrases You Use

In no small way, how you converse may convey issues from your previous lives. Write down all the phrases or words that you repeatedly use; then after each one, use your imagination to come up with a past life that might fit your current sayings or explain why you choose the words you speak.

- What phrases do you often repeat? What's occurring in your life when you begin to use each phrase?

- What words do say over and over? Pay attention to what's happening to you or what you're feeling when you catch yourself repeating these words.

- What phrases or words do you really dislike that other people use? What kinds of emotions or images come into your mind when you hear them?

Body Type

It's not uncommon for certain physical features to reemerge lifetime after lifetime. Objectively examine your body and write down all the discernible features that you possess.

- What is you body type? Is it slender, frail, muscular, athletic, portly, or small?

- Do you possess any unusual physical features? Were you born with them, or did they develop later in life? Do you recall any

images associated with them? If so, what
might they have been?

- What judgments do you believe others
  make about you simply by how you look?
  Would you consider these assessments
  accurate?

- Do you feel comfortable in your skin?
  Does your body *not* fit who you feel you
  truly are?

- If there was a time in history or a part of the
  world where people might have had bodies
  similar to yours, where might it have been?

Health Issues

Simply focusing intently on the part of your body
that's chronically out of balance can often ignite images
from the past.

- Did you have any recurring health issues
  during childhood? What was your emotional response to health concerns when
  you were a child? Patient? Bored? Upset?
  Sad? Lonely? Angry?

- Do you have any physical handicaps or
  disabilities? What reason have you given
  yourself for these limitations? Do you have
  a sense that there's an underlying explanation as well? What might that be?

- Have you ever had any pain that couldn't be medically accounted for? Where in your body was it? What was happening in your life at the same time?

- Is your eyesight good? Are you nearsighted or farsighted? Is there something in your life that you'd prefer not to see?

- How is your hearing? Is there anything that you'd rather not listen to?

- How are your teeth? Are you able to really *sink your teeth* into life situations?

- Have you always believed that you'd live a long life? Why? Alternatively, have you thought that your life would be short? Why?

- What emotional responses do you have to your current and past health challenges?

- Is your health generally good, or do you constantly struggle to stay in balance? Do you have a chronic condition?

- Are you committed to alternative-health remedies or to allopathic medicine? If you seek holistic methods, do you respond well to Chinese herbs and acupuncture, Western herbs, Ayurvedic massage, hydrotherapy, cleansing steams, colonics, or crystal therapy? (Often the type of treatment that works the best for you—or the worst—is a reflection of a past-life remedy.)

- Do you follow a special diet? If so, what is it? Was there a time in history when people ate in a similar way?

- What part of your body has chronic challenges? If there was some traumatic event from the past associated with this, what might it be?

Scars, Birthmarks, and Tattoos

Birthmarks and scars can often be linked to your previous lives. Look over your entire body and write down any that you have. Draw an outline of your body and indicate exactly where they are—note even the smallest ones. Pay particular attention to areas that have been scarred several times in the exact same places. A simple guided meditation into the area of a recurrent scar (or birthmark) can often reveal past-life memories.

- Where are the scars on your body? How did you get them? Do you have any emotions associated with them?

- How old were you were when you obtained your scars? What else was occurring in your life at the same time?

- Do you have any scars that you don't know where they came from?

- If you have a birthmark, where is it on your body? How big is it and what shape is it in?

- Does your birthmark resemble anything?

- If you have tattoos, are they from any particular culture or specific era?

Injuries, Diseases, and Surgeries

Your feelings about injuries and diseases that you've had can contain valuable information on your search for who you were. The mishaps that your body has encountered aren't usually an accident. List every injury, disease, and surgery that you've ever had. Then write down the emotions that each one brings up for you. Notice if there is any similarity in the feelings that arise.

- Have you had any recurring injuries in a particular place on your body? If there was a soul drama that might account for that specific injury, what might it be?

- Are there any diseases that you're terrified of contracting? Do you have an unaccountable fear of germs or bacteria?

- Have you had any unusual diseases or illnesses? What part of your body was affected?

- What kinds of surgeries have you had?
  Why? Did the medical procedure heal the
  condition? What else was occurring in your
  life at the time?

Dreams

Your dreams can be a secret doorway into your past.
Take the time to write down and record them—even if
you can only recall a few snippets—because that information might help you connect to your previous lives.
When you've amassed many fragments, try to expand
them into a full scenario. This method can work well to
begin to gain insights as to who you were.

- As a child, did you have any recurring
  dreams or nightmares?

- Have you ever had a dream that was so real
  you felt that you were there? What were
  your surroundings? Were you located in
  another historical period?

- Does there seem to be a theme in your
  dreams? For example, are you always the
  victim, or are you usually the antagonist
  or perpetrator? Are you constantly running
  away from something?

- Do you regularly assume a specific role in
  your dreams? For example, are you usually
  the mother, teacher, or laborer?

Putting the Pieces of the Puzzle Together

Once you've answered all the questions and compiled lists of clues, study this information and you'll be able to piece together the puzzle, forming a picture of some of your past-life scenarios. It's not uncommon for people who do this exercise to have spontaneous former-life memories. Trust in the process. These kinds of memories arise when the time is right for you to process and heal them. *Have faith that the time is right.* Notice—and write down—any similarity or connection between these recollections and your current life.

As a suggestion, write each of the topics listed in this chapter on top of a separate sheet of paper in your past-life detective journal. As you answer the questions below each subject heading, write down all the "clues" that you can gather. You may want to place the completed sheets side by side so that a larger picture can begin to form.

When I did this exercise, I saw that I had amassed evidence indicating a past life in Japan. I've always loved the simple lines of traditional Japanese architecture. In my current life, not only did I live for more than two years in a Japanese Buddhist monastery, but I also studied this culture while I was attending the University of Hawaii. I've also learned about the Japanese tea ceremony and *ikebana* (flower arranging) and trained in the healing systems of Reiki and shiatsu. In addition, my favorite restaurants have always been Japanese! And to top it off, there was a period in my life when I saw every samurai movie that was available—at that time, I held Toshiro Mifune in the same regard as people who revere Johnny Depp today. Looking at these clues as my own *reincarnation detective,* it makes sense that I had a past life in the Far East.

As you create your lists, pay attention to your emotional responses regarding each topic. For example, under the "Animal and Pets" heading, be sure to note if there's a particular animal you have an emotional affinity for or perhaps one that you've always been afraid of. I know a man who has a very close attachment to horses. He was a Mongolian in a past life and during that time, he loved his horse even more than his wife. In the category "Personality Traits, Mannerisms, and Habitual Behaviors," examine any personal quirks that you may have. I met a woman who rubs her throat whenever she feels stress. In a previous life, she discovered that she'd been stabbed in the throat; and in her current life, any kind of stress subconsciously activates her past-life memory.

Patterns will start to emerge as you gather your clues. You may ask yourself, *How will I know if I'm accurate? How can I distinguish between simple fascination and a stirring of deep, inner knowing?* A good indication is usually your emotional response. If it feels right, it probably is. If you're unsure, meditate upon the ideas that are beginning to form from your insights. Even if you're not completely clear, sooner or later your subconscious will show you the path to greater understanding. In particular, watch your dreams after you've finished answering the questions in this chapter. Past-life memories often begin to unfold during your nighttime hours. Once you've completed this exercise, you're ready for past-life regression.

Chapter Six

REGRESSION . . .
A JOURNEY OF
TRANSFORMATION

You're now ready to try your own regression. It is a profound journey into self-awareness. Embarking on a past-life odyssey not only allows you to see who you've been, but in a deeper sense, it will connect you to the true essence of your soul. The more you practice these exercises—and the more past-life experiences you become aware of and resolve—the greater balance you'll achieve in your current life.

The most important aspect of past-life regression is to enjoy yourself . . . and you can increase your enjoyment by not being overly serious as you examine who you were. It helps to look at each life as a role that you performed in a play—you're no longer that character, no more than you're a coat that you take off when you enter your home. You are an infinite, eternal being and every past life is just a part you played in order to learn and grow spiritually . . . in truth, *the role is not who you truly are.*

Remembering Your Past Selves

Almost everyone who goes through a past-life regression is touched by the images, memories, and emotions that surface; and no matter how fleeting they may be, transformative changes occur almost mystically in the lives of those individuals. Simply beginning to examine your past lives—even if at first they're just snippets of memories—initiates powerful healing and releases limitations.

As your memories from the past begin to be revealed in your regressions, you may only gain small fragments or ephemeral images. It may feel like a subtle echo of a recollection at the edge of your mind, but you just can't quite remember it; or you may see a quick flash of a memory, but you can't fully grasp it. Sometimes instead of a visual impression, you may have an emotional response or a visceral experience, for your body subconsciously holds the memories of all your previous lives. Be conscious of every thought, feeling, and image—no matter how seemingly insignificant—because each may offer a valuable key to unlock your past.

Also be aware that in your early attempts to discover prior incarnations, the images might be jumbled—just like trying to remember instances from your childhood.

Sometimes there's an overlap in which images from one life merge with another. For example, you might witness a Roman chariot flying through the dust and yet there's a hot air balloon overhead. This doesn't mean that what you're seeing isn't valid; it's just an indication that two lives have collided. However, the more you practice, the clearer and less disordered the memories will become. Also, as you accumulate past-life clues and complete the following exercises, a more accurate picture will begin to unfold.

Using the Power of Creative Visualization for Your Past-Life Journey

The most common method of past-life regression involves using your powers of visualization and practicing what shamans call *journeying*. Visualization is an excellent technique because it allows you to reach the subconscious. It's medically and scientifically recognized that visualized scenarios actually bring about psychological and even physiological changes—in some cases to almost the same degree as direct experience.

A study at the University of Chicago demonstrated the power of visualization. Student volunteers were divided into three groups, and their basketball shooting abilities were noted. After each group underwent a different kind of preparation, every individual was observed shooting foul shots. (A foul shot, or free throw, is when a player stands on a set line and is allowed an unhindered attempt to shoot a basket. The distance between the hoop and the player is always the same, and the action of the game is halted while the player shoots.) Group One didn't practice foul shots for the 30 days of the experiment, and at the end of that time they showed no improvement. Group Two practiced foul shots every day for 30 days and showed a 24 percent improvement. Group Three practiced foul shots for 30 days *only in their minds* and showed an astonishing 23 percent improvement.

The significance of this phenomenon can be applied to past-life therapy. If you visualize a journey to a past life *and resolve it*, your subconscious will recognize that inner journey as a real one—and it will recognize *and accept* the resolution that you've come to as a real one.

Which of My Lifetimes Will Emerge?

When doing past-life processes, you'll become aware *only* of the incarnations that reflect something that you're also dealing with in your present life. Whatever lifetime you see will contain the people, situations, or issues that symbolize those in your life now. Wherever you are at any point in your current existence mirrors one or only a couple of particular past lives, and you'll usually be surrounded or closely involved with individuals from those lifetimes. In the future, you may be influenced by completely different previous incarnations.

For example, Sarah became absorbed by her spiritual path and started to become involved with her local church. She began to assist at the Sunday morning children's group and developed a number of new friendships within the congregation. At the same time, she developed a fascination with candles and incense. In a past-life regression, she discovered that she'd been a nun in the south of France—where they'd burned many candles and used incense—and realized that her new church friends had all been nuns at the same abbey. In their shared past life, they'd cared for orphaned children. They were drawn together once again in similar circumstances in order to resolve any karmic blockages they may have accrued in their past lives. When Sarah balanced the karma from that experience, she moved on to other interests.

Isn't Everyone Cleopatra?

Contrary to skeptics of regression, rarely is anyone famous. In fact, out of the thousands of people I've regressed in my private sessions and group regressions, almost no one was a well-known figure from history. The majority are ordinary individuals facing the challenges that have emerged throughout the course of humanity: hunger, wars, migration, disease, political upheaval, and survival amid the elements. The lives that you encounter will be filled with the same obstacles that people have confronted throughout time. (And I have yet to meet the reincarnation of Cleopatra.)

Feeling Safe

To ensure that your regression is a positive experience, pick an emotionally and physically comfortable place in your home where you can do it. Select a time when you're not overwhelmed by external stresses. You may also want someone you care about and trust to be present and ready to talk to you after the process, if you feel you might need such assistance. This can be helpful not only for dealing with past-life issues that are negative, but also for sorting out the positive ones. A good discussion with a close friend can be extremely valuable for gaining a clear perspective and piecing together an entire picture from fragments of information.

As I mentioned earlier, it's important that you thoroughly familiarize yourself with the techniques described in this book before you try out any of the full-regression processes. It's vital to learn ways to resolve the experiences you may encounter in a past life in order to heal. You don't want to just relive your previous scenarios—you want to unravel and settle them. Just knowing that you have the tools to do so will give you a feeling of safety.

The Inner Voyage . . .
a Past-Life Visualization Technique

To use this visualization technique for past-life regression, you may want to create a recording for yourself to listen to as you practice. You could also ask a friend to read aloud a script that you've created, or simply imagine yourself on this sacred journey. Here's a summary of the steps in The Inner Voyage.

Step 1: The Sanctuary. Relax and then imagine yourself in a peaceful place in nature. This step is essential for your ultimate outcome.

Step 2: The Transition from Present to Past. Shift out of the imagined place in nature into a neutral middle ground before actually experiencing a past life. The transition stage provides the means to enter into your distant past.

Step 3: The Past Life. This is the stage where you actually experience who you were in one of your incarnations.

Step 4: Resolving Issues. During this stage, you release your attachment to that life, enter the sanctity of the spirit world, and examine and resolve issues from that past incarnation.

Step 1: The Sanctuary

To begin your visual journey to your past, first allow yourself to become very relaxed. (My guided-relaxation and past-life regression meditations are available through **www.hayhouse.com** and iTunes.) Then imagine going to a place in nature; this can be either a made-up setting or somewhere you've actually been where you've felt at peace. This is your sanctuary—a place where you feel safe and grounded.

If you have difficulty visualizing, as some people do, I suggest that you get a *sense* of being in the natural world, using your other sense organs. To do so, you might imagine the sounds around you: birds singing, a faraway waterfall, the babble of a brook, and so on. Try to really perceive what scents and physical sensations you might experience. For example, if you imagine yourself in the woods, can you smell the dampness of spongy moss under your feet? Does the aroma of fresh air and pine trees clear your head? Can you feel the warmth of the sun penetrate your body as you walk along, or perhaps as you lie stretched out on a smooth sun-baked rock?

Visualizing yourself in nature will help you become calm and serene before going on to your past-life regression. You'll feel the connection with the earth, and this provides great comfort to many people. This is also an excellent time to contact your guides or guardian angel. (Spirit guides and angels will be discussed in more detail in Chapter 9.) The sanctuary increases your feeling of safety and well-being before stepping into the past.

Step 2: The Transition from Present to Past

Once you've imagined a place in nature, it's important to have a transition time before delving into a previous life. You'll be traveling a long way into your past, so you can think of the transition as a kind of gentle vehicle that will carry you wherever you want to go, ensuring a safe arrival with minimal culture shock. You need such a mechanism in order to let your mind and body adjust to the suspension of linear time and space. Here are some methods that can help you make a successful transition, which is the first stage to the regression exercises. Choose the technique that feels best to you.

Time Tunnel. Leave your safe place (or nature sanctuary) and walk into a time tunnel. You might count the steps or imagine getting closer and closer until you finally step into a past life.

Bridge of Time. While you're in nature, a bridge appears before you. Climb up its ascending steps high above the clouds. As you continue your journey, descend down the bridge back through the clouds and into a past life.

River of Time. Climb into a small boat lined with soft pillows. Lie down and watch the clouds overhead as the boat travels of its own volition through the river of time, taking you to a past life.

Cosmic Elevator. Step into the cosmic elevator. Every floor number on the lighted panel represents a different lifetime. You can either push a button or wait for the elevator to stop. When the doors open, you enter a past life.

Mystical Door. Imagine what the mystical door looks like, feels like, and even what sound it makes when you knock on it. When it opens, a past life is revealed.

Room of Doors. Enter a circular room with many doors or walk down a hallway lined with doors on either side. Each one opens to one of your past lives. If you'd like, imagine small windows to look through in each doorway before you turn the knob and step inside.

Time Machine. A time machine appears in your sanctuary. You enter it and the machine lifts up into the clouds. When it descends, you're in a past life. You can even have a panel inside that shows you the exact date you've arrived in.

Mists of Time. Your serene place in nature becomes very misty. As you walk into the mists, you know that an amazing transition is occurring. You experience a metamorphosis, and although you can't see it happening, you feel yourself changing as it transforms into the physical body you occupied in a previous life. Then you step into the past.

Soul Garden. The transition area is a splendid garden. One area is made up of fertile soil where dreams can be planted; and another section is where relationships grow, and every person you know is there represented as a plant or flower. In another part of the garden, flowers symbolize your talents and abilities. A different area is set aside for future possibilities. Also within this garden is a magical entrance point leading to your past lives. It might be the old garden shed that dwells at the center of the garden.

Magical Theater. Imagine that you've entered a large and beautiful theater where a number of movies are showing. Each of these films allows you to explore a past life. You can choose to enter by stepping into the screen, or you may decide to sit back and watch your past life from the safe perspective of a comfortable theater seat. Additionally, you can watch actors portray your past lives just as if you were in an actual theater.

Mystical Computer Room. You're in a large, lighted laboratory where there are complex and specialized computers. You can program them to offer you personal guidance or search for information on the Cosmic Internet regarding your past lives. Alternatively, you can "Google" your past lives.

The Doorkeeper. In your safe place in nature, you encounter a wise and gentle being. This is the Doorkeeper, a past-life guide who knows all about you, loves you very much, and is able to safely guide you wherever you need to go. You can ask this being any questions about your past; and this wise being can lead you back to a previous life, into a future one, or even to another realm. Your kind guide might also present you with a gift that will be useful in your past-life journeys.

Other Transitions. There are endless variations on these exercises. Try them out to see which ones work best for you. Here are a few more ideas:

- Magical Time Bubble
- Transporter (think *Star Trek*)
- Holodeck (think *Star Trek*)
- Mystical Train
- Through the Vortex (recall *Sliders* or *Stargate*)
- Quantum Leap
- Small Plane That Travels Through Time
- Closets of Abilities or Room of Costumes
- Bazaar with Tents That Open to Different Realms (similar to *Harry Potter*)
- Book of Life (with moving pictures)
- Hall of Akashic Records
- Ancient Library of Time

Step 3: The Past Life

After you successfully transition from your sanctuary in nature, the next step is to actually visualize a previous life. Once you've gone through a metamorphosis into your past-life body, take a moment to look down at your feet and notice where you're standing. Observe the shoes you're wearing or the coverings on your feet. Do they appear to be male or female, young or old? Ask yourself, *Am I indoors or outdoors?* If you're outside, what does the landscape look like? Be aware of noises, smells, and physical sensations; most of all, be cognizant of your emotional state. Once you begin to get a sense of where you are—and who you are—you can explore that life. (At any time you desire, you can immediately slip out of this past life, and return to the present time.)

Step 4: Resolving Issues

Once you've completed your exploration, imagine yourself floating out of that body and entering a beautiful, peaceful spirit world where you can review the past incarnation you've just experienced. While in the safety of the ethereal realm, you're also able to release old patterns, forgive others or accept self-forgiveness, and reconnect with the Creator. To do this, first review the past life you've just visited with an air of sacred detachment. Understand that everything you've experienced in that incarnation was for your development as a soul. Ask yourself, *What did I learn during the turning points in that life, and what was the meaning of each event?* When you feel complete, imagine that you're radiating love and joy to that lifetime from your vantage point in the realm of spirit.

The Inner Voyage Meditation

This sample meditation shows how to put all four of The Inner Voyage steps together. Ask a friend to read it aloud to you, or you could also record yourself reading the process and play it back anytime you'd like. (If you're making your own recording, substitute "I" for "you.")

Start by getting your body into a relaxed position, either sitting or reclining. Now take some very deep breaths. With each breath you take and each sound you hear, you become more and more relaxed.

Put your attention on your left foot and feel it completely let go. Allow a delicious wave of relaxation to slowly roll from your feet up through your hips to your torso, stretching through your arms and hands, and up and out of the top of your head. Your entire body is now relaxed, warm, and comfortable. Take one deep breath, totally surrender, and let go.

Imagine that you're walking across a field. It's a sunny day and you're filled with the deep scent of lush summer grasses. You hear the soft drone of insects and the merry songs of birds . . . these sounds fill the air with a soothing, rhythmic cadence. A mist begins to rise from the field and stillness fills the air. In the distance, you hear a gentle river lapping against the bank. As you approach, the mist becomes very thick. At the water's edge, you notice a sturdy bridge crossing it. This is the Bridge of Time.

The mist has become so thick that you can't make out the other side of the bridge; in fact, you can only see a few feet in front of you as you step onto it. With each step you take, you know you're nearing one of your past lives.

I shall count from 1 to 10. When I reach the end, you'll step off the bridge at a time long ago, before you came into your present body. Although you can't see, you begin to feel yourself changing as you shape-shift into the body that you occupied in a previous incarnation. I'll begin now: 1-2-3-4 . . . with each step you take, the swirling, mystical mist seems to embrace you with warmth and love . . . 5-6-7 . . . you're aware of a loving presence guiding and protecting your every step . . . 8-9 . . . the fog is beginning to thin, the end of the bridge is near . . . 10 . . . step off the bridge.

You've arrived in one of your past lives. The mist has completely cleared. Look down at your feet. Are they the feet of a man or a woman? Are they young or old looking? Are you outside or inside? What surface are you standing on? Sand? Stone? Tile? Wooden floor? Grass? What covering do you have on your feet? What type of clothing are you wearing? Do you feel more male or female? Are you young, old, or middle-aged? Look around and note your surroundings. Are you in the country or the city? If there are any buildings, pay attention to the architecture. Are there any people nearby? If there are, listen to them speaking. What language does it sound like? Is there anyone who resembles a person from your present life? As you wander around and perceive this life, tune in to your emotions. How does this life feel? You have a few minutes to explore. Be willing to use your imagination. You may begin now.

Go to a time in this life that was very significant or important to you. You have a short while to experience what's happening and to determine how you feel about these circumstances. Continue to move forward in time in the past life that you're exploring . . . go onward to the moment when you're about to shed your body and pass over to the spirit world. How did you die? Was it slowly or suddenly? What people were around you? Were you reluctant or glad to go? From a spiritual view, the process of dying is seldom recognized as a painful event, and there's usually a great sigh of relief once you realize that you've passed over. It's like returning home after a long absence. You have a minute to observe this event in your past life. You may do this now.

Go forward into the spirit world. From your perspective in the spirit world, what did you learn from the past life? Were there any fears or concerns from there that are still present in your life today?

As you discover where these fears originated, you now know that they aren't real, and it's simple to release them. Just let go. You know that you can create your life in the present to be exactly the way you want it. You can choose freely without programming from other lives.

Now it's time to let all of this fade away and return to your current life. Just let the past life fade away . . . just drift away.

As you move closer to normal waking awareness, you feel strong and empowered. You've stepped into your far past with courage and have looked at who and what you were. With this examination, your present life is enhanced and you've taken a step closer to the divinity within you. In the future, you're free to explore any past life, and the knowledge you gain creates the space for your life to be more fulfilling and whole.

I'm going to count from 1 to 5. When I reach 5, you'll be totally awake and aware . . . 1-2 . . . your body is healthy and strong . . . 3 . . . more and more alert . . . 4 . . . your eyes feel as if they've been bathed in fresh, cooling springwater . . . 5 . . . wide awake and feeling great. Open your eyes now. Stretch and enjoy the beauty of the day.

You can use The Inner Voyage Meditation again and again, or you can create your own past-life journeys using the methods described earlier in the chapter. You might want to try it right before bed, as this will encourage past-life recall in your dreams.

Body Wisdom . . . a Sensory Past-Life Regression Technique

This method is especially valuable for someone who is very kinesthetic. It's a technique based on the idea that your memories, beliefs, and judgments all exist in your body, so by tuning in to your body, you can activate the associated past-life memories. There are four steps to this technique:

Step 1: Declare the Problem. The first step is to pin-point exactly what you want to heal, change, or understand in your life. The clearer you are about what you'd like to transform, the easier it will be for it to occur.

Step 2: Locate the Body Sensation. Almost all of the challenges in your life can be traced to hidden memories and life decisions made during those times . . . and these are stored in your body as well as in your mind. In this second step, you take time to discover and explore the secret places within where emotions, sensations, and memories associated with the difficulties reside.

Step 3: Activate Spontaneous Past-Life Memories. Simply by focusing your awareness and attention on a specific body area, decisions and limiting beliefs from the past will often spontaneously begin to arise.

Step 4: Resolve Past-Life Blockages. Change past-life scenarios that were difficult or traumatic in order to create positive outcomes. You're not stuck with the past, and it doesn't have to dictate your future.

Step 1: Declare the Problem

Start by selecting which parts of your life you'd like assistance with. Be as specific as possible. Remember, not all problems have their source in a previous incarnation. But if you can't seem to find a cause in your current life, you'll often find the roots in the far past. Here are some areas that you may consider in order to see what the past-life connection could be.

Relationship difficulties. The most severe relationship or family challenges you've had are most often a result of unresolved issues from your past lives. You're together again with the same individuals to work it out during this life. There can be issues of betrayal, old supposed scores to settle, arrogance, injustice, power struggles, abuse, and so on.

Abundance issues. These can come from abuse of money or power in the past; alternatively, they can come from vows of poverty.

Health issues. Past-life physical or emotional trauma that was never addressed or healed could result in current health issues. Heart problems can come from a broken heart in a past life; arthritis could be from rigidity in a past incarnation; and throat problems may be due to strangulation, being the victim of hanging, or not speaking up.

Fears or phobias. I've found that almost all unaccounted and unexplained phobias or fears have their root in a trauma from a past life.

Forgiveness of others. If there's any unresolved anger or resentment about the way you were treated in a previous incarnation, it can arise as the inability to forgive others in your current life.

Forgiveness of yourself. If you acted without honor in the past, this can manifest in the present as the inability to forgive yourself—even over matters that aren't your fault or that are inconsequential.

Fear of speaking your truth. This often comes from lifetimes in which you were censured or severely punished for speaking up for yourself or sharing your beliefs.

Accidents. Especially if you've been injured in the same place more than once, accidents can be a reenactment of battlefield injuries or even symbolic of the manner in which you've met your death in a previous incarnation.

Blockages in your life. This can be any area in which you feel stymied and can't seem to get ahead. For example, an inability to lose weight may be a current blockage but can be traced to a past life of gluttony or even starvation. If you sabotage potential relationships, it could be attributed to a former life filled with rejection, callousness, or loneliness.

Fear of abandonment. Perhaps you were abandoned, orphaned, or separated from loved ones during a migration or war, or maybe you sold people into slavery or tore families apart.

Insecurity. Feelings of insecurity can be caused by past-life arrogance or by having had a demeaning life in which you were unhappy.

Guilt or shame. This can come from deep guilt about something that you did, such as being responsible for the death or betrayal of someone whom you cared about or being in charge of something that resulted in the suffering of others.

Sexual challenges. Impotence, difficulty becoming pregnant, and other sexual or physical blockages can often arise from past-life rape or abuse.

Talents or strengths you want to reawaken. In addition to releasing negative patterns, you can also use this process to activate talents and abilities that you had in the past but don't currently possess.

Step 2: Locate the Body Sensation

Once you've identified the specific issue in your life that you want to work on, then just relax and allow yourself to be aware of what emotion, attitude, or feeling you associate with your area of concern. (For example, let's say that you're afraid to swim or get into large bodies of water, such as a lake or ocean, and you want to release this blockage so that you can enjoy swimming. The emotion that you associate with this concern might be fear.) Imagine that you're feeling the emotion right now. (To *feel* emotions, locate where they are in your body. Fear may feel like a tightening sensation in the center of your chest, or perhaps every time you're afraid you hold your breath.)

Go through your body and locate the area where you strongly feel the emotion associated with your issue. Where does it reside? Here's an example of how this works: Maybe you've been angry with your father for mistreating you during childhood, but now you want to forgive him. Think about your father and the mistreatment you suffered. Feel the anger. Use your imagination to travel inside your body and find the spot where you *feel* the rage most intensely. If it feels like a lump in your chest, focus your entire attention there and ask yourself what this sensation might look like. Use the following criteria:

- Color
- Size
- Shape
- Texture

To understand how to do this, imagine that you can "see" the emotions inside your body. What color(s) might they be? Repeat the process for size, shape, and texture. For instance, your anger at your father might "look" oblong, dark blue, and about the size of a football; it resides in the center of your chest.

Answering questions about the color, size, shape, and texture helps activate the past-life memories in your body by focusing attention on the area where they're stored. This is a powerful technique because these ancient memories are lodged not just in your brain, but also within your physical self. Using the body is an excellent way to access previous incarnations.

Step 3: Activate Spontaneous Past-Life Memories

Keeping your awareness on the particular place in your body that you've chosen, notice any spontaneous memories that surface. If the memories are from last week rather than a past life, that's all right. Ask to see earlier, similar images. Continue regressing until you reach a memory that seems to be the likely source of your difficulty. If you aren't sensing anything, go even deeper into this part of your physical self. (You might imagine that you're very small and that you're actually inside that specific part in your body.) Ask yourself, *If I was aware of a memory, what might it be?* Give your imagination full rein.

Step 4: Resolve Past-Life Blockages

If any uncomfortable memories arise, either change the meaning that you give those events or manipulate the scenario so that it has a positive outcome. This step is very important! You should feel great at the completion of this process, for the blockage has finally been resolved. (We'll discuss resolving past-life difficulties in more detail in Chapter 8.)

Group Regression for Past-Life Recall

Most of my regression work is now conducted with big groups—usually from 100 to 500 people at a time. I find this setting effective because there's a tremendous amount of energy available in a large gathering of individuals. If you choose to be regressed among others, it's vital that the person leading the process has many years of experience and is someone you feel good about. I recommend that you attain personal references from those who have previously attended the particular seminar you're considering. Participating in a group regression can be exhilarating because of the remarkable synchronicity and coincidences that often occur.

Regression Tapes and CDs

Some people use regression tapes and CDs quite successfully. The first time I recorded my regression techniques, the engineer in the recording booth—who didn't believe in past lives—fell off his stool and spontaneously connected with a past life! (If you'd like to obtain my past-life regression tapes, CDs, or videos, please visit my Website: **www.DeniseLinn.com**.)

Past-Life Coach

Some issues in life call for the help of a past-life coach, but other situations may require a licensed therapist. An indication that you need the assistance of a therapist or psychologist is if the feelings you're experiencing are interfering with your ability to go about your normal life. If you feel completely overwhelmed and can't cope, get help from a professional therapist, psychologist, or counselor. The first step is to seek references from people you trust. It's also a good idea to check the certification and credentials of the therapist you choose.

However, if your life is in pretty good shape but you'd like to gain a deeper understanding of who you are, then you might want to consult a past-life coach or regression practitioner. (Visit **www.DeniseLinn.com** or **www.Soul-Coaching.com** for referrals.)

Enjoy the Process

Remember to have fun in your past-life explorations! Enjoy the process and let go of concerns about always being historically correct—this makes it easier for your subconscious mind to bring up past-life memories. If you're constantly questioning the validity of the events of a previous incarnation, you can lose the psychological value of your exploration and it becomes more difficult to recall your past life accurately. It would be similar to trying to remember your present-life 12th birthday party. If your conscious mind kept saying, "No, that can't be right," it would become increasingly difficult to recall that day.

Through the use of regression exercises, you can open the door to the past and begin to release limitations in order to have a more beautiful, loving future. Exploration of your earlier incarnations will help you gain an unparalleled understanding into your present-life circumstances.

Chapter Seven

DREAMS AND PAST LIVES

*"The question of karma is obscure to me, as is also
the problem of personal rebirth. . . . Recently, however,
I observed in myself a series of dreams which would
seem to describe the process of reincarnation."*
— Carl Jung, from *Memories, Dreams, Reflections*

It's widely accepted that dreams can offer potent insights into your life. These mysterious messages from your mind can warn you of danger, or they may contain seeds for creative inspiration. Einstein stated that his theory of relativity came to him in a dream; in fact, he declared that many of his discoveries were the results of his nighttime reveries.

Dreams can serve as a gateway to the mystic arenas of your inner realms. They can be a springboard for night healing, astral travel, and soul-searching. These nocturnal visions can foretell the future and give you valuable information about the past. They are a viable way for your guides to communicate directly with you without having to pass the censor of your conscious mind. Dreams can also be a doorway to travel through time and space in order to step into a past life.

D. Scott Rogo, who was a faculty member of John F. Kennedy University in California, conducted some interesting research regarding visions of reincarnation in dreams. He placed advertisements in metaphysical-oriented magazines to elicit responses from anyone who had experienced past-life memories other than through regression methods. In his book *The Search for Yesterday,* Rogo reported that the largest group of credible recollections of past lives came from dreams.

When we're dreaming, our mind is much less likely to be confined by the limits of logic, which is why it's often the easiest way to connect with our past lives. Even people who don't believe in reincarnation have reported dreams in which they've participated in activities that took place during another time in history. This can, of course, be attributed to a recently viewed movie or a book we've just read. However, there are some qualities that distinguish past-life dreams from ordinary ones.

Dreams that feature previous incarnations seem much more real than conventional dreams; the colors are brighter, edges and corners appear sharper, and everything seems much more vivid and clear. Frederick Lenz, a psychologist with the New School for Social Research, reports in his book *Lifetimes* that many of his subjects were aware and strongly affected when their dreams were of former lives. When past-life dreams recur, as they often do, there's usually an unresolved issue that's desperately trying to filter through to the consciousness. These dreams can be interpreted as an invitation for us to resolve that past-life conflict or difficulty.

Dreams, Past Lives, and the New Harmonics

In the next few years, I believe there will be a huge increase in the number of visions from previous incarnations that appear in our dreams, and they'll act as a filtering ground for ancient issues that are influencing our present and struggling to reach resolution.

Here's a metaphor I use to explain why our dreams are so important for resolving past-life issues. Imagine the midnight darkness of a desert. Shimmering stars punctuate the sky, as cars below wind their way along a solitary road. Most of the people driving are enjoying the silent beauty of the night; however, a few have their radios turned on, but because they're miles away from the local stations they can't pick up anything. Then from the farthest reaches of the universe, a CRS (Cosmic Radio Station) begins to broadcast to Earth.

Those with their radios on hear muffled static, as waves of increasingly higher frequencies are projected to our planet. As the intensity rises, the static also becomes louder until the signals are fine-tuned and clear. Then all mental and physical tensions ease completely, and all those who are listening hear the most exquisite music—sounds so soothing and beautiful that cares and concerns begin to fade away. The irritations and difficulties of life dissolve, and there's a feeling of infinite peace. The very special music from CRS stirs up a remembrance in the depths of the soul of a distant place . . . a place filled with an abundance of light, compassion, and fulfillment.

Right now, new frequencies and energies are flooding our planet. For many, their dreams are becoming like a turned-on radio. Because of the nonsequential, intuitive nature of dreams, you'll first "hear" many of the "CRS" frequencies through the symbols and images you perceive while sleeping. Your nighttime reveries are an untapped source of enormous potential for the planetary release that's occurring.

In the months and years ahead, many past-life visions may appear in your dreams. These new harmonics will stimulate old blockages that have resided deep within you for lifetimes. You may even feel as if your life is filled with static, and as strange as it sounds, this is a good thing because it means that your "radio" is on. (There are many people who blithely go about their seemingly static-free lives; unfortunately, because they don't have their "radios" on, they may never hear the exquisite music or experience the profound energy that you eventually will.) As these blockages are released, you'll begin to remember who you are . . . and the static will begin to ease, metamorphosing into a beauty you've never known before.

Dreaming of the Holocaust

When I was a child, I had a recurring nightmare. There was a furnace with its door open, and I could see the bright fire and feel the intense heat as I watched the dead bodies of adults and children being placed into the flames. Every morning I'd wake up feeling horrified over what I'd witnessed during the night.

I was very concerned about these childhood dreams, and in my early 20s I consulted a psychologist who said that my nightmares meant that I'd harbored feelings of jealousy toward my younger brothers and sister. I was the eldest of four children. He said that as my siblings were born, I was consciously helpful and loving. However, subconsciously, I wanted to get rid of them—by throwing them into a furnace. At the time, this sounded like a good theory and since I wasn't having the nightmares anymore, I was content with the doctor's interpretation.

You hear what you need to hear at any given time in your life; you create what you need when you need it. *You can't hear the truth until you're truly ready to listen.*

Many years passed (more than 40 since my childhood nightmares), and I was in London. I decided to get a massage; the practitioner was a remarkable man and I felt that when he worked on me he wasn't just soothing my body, he was also reaching into my soul.

In the middle of the session he paused abruptly, looked at me, and said, "You died in Auschwitz."

"Excuse me?" I asked.

"You died at Auschwitz."

Shocked, I replied, "I don't think that's something I'd forget." (It was also not the sort of thing this man would normally have said to anyone, but somehow he felt compelled to say this to me at that moment.)

I explained to him that as a past-life therapist I was familiar with my previous incarnations and wouldn't have forgotten a life as monumental as that! As surprised

as I was by his revelation, I was perhaps even more startled by my curt, almost rude, response.

Very sweetly and humbly, he said, "All right . . .
maybe I was wrong," and continued the massage. But
something shook inside me—the way a volcano shakes a
mountain at its base. I thought of my childhood nightmare and how people had often called me a "Jewish
mother," even though that isn't my ethnic background.
I remembered the abject terror I'd felt when I arrived at
the German border and had to show my papers before
entering the country to present some lectures. I recalled
the deep compassion I've always felt for anyone who's
been unjustly imprisoned.

I walked around in a daze. Had I been Jewish in my
last life? Did I die at Auschwitz? Why didn't I remember it or have any visual images? I didn't talk to anyone
about my experience. My pride as a past-life therapist
wouldn't even allow me to consider that I could have
had a life in Nazi Germany and forgotten—it was too
unbelievable.

A few months later, during a break in a seminar I was
leading, a man from the Netherlands talked to me about
growing up there during the war. He told me about being
a young boy in Amsterdam, when he and his mother
were interrogated at length. His mother was taken away
to a prison camp, and he never saw her again.

Suddenly, in a voice that seemed not to come from
me, I said, "I knew your mother. She was thinking of you
before she died. She loved you very, very much."

This man and I began to sob uncontrollably. I was
stunned by what I'd said because I still hadn't had any
memories of being at Auschwitz, yet something even deeper
than visual images responded to his story. Somewhere

inside me, I knew that I'd spoken the truth—I was there. I did know his mother. And life had come full circle so that the promise I'd made to her—to tell her son that she loved him until the end—was fulfilled. *The vows we make are extraordinarily powerful, transcending time and space.*

Concerned that I still couldn't recall a past life in a prison camp, and unable to regress myself back to that time, I began to ask friends about their past lives to see if I could gain any clues. On a subsequent trip to Australia, I had lunch with a woman who had lived with us in Seattle for three years. She, too, was a past-life regressionist. I asked, "Do you remember if you had a lifetime in connection with Nazi Germany?"

She replied, "Oh, I thought you knew. I was a prison warden at Auschwitz. I've always been fascinated by German culture. I studied German and even lived in the country as a young woman. In fact, as a child I read *Mein Kampf* nine times!"

Suddenly, I remembered that this woman used to wear shiny black boots all the time . . . and I recalled how much I disliked them. (After the first edition of this book came out, under the title *Past Lives, Present Dreams*, I received a poignant letter from a Hasidic rabbi, Yonassan Gershom—*Hasidism* is an Orthodox branch of Judaism. Gershom had written a book called *From Ashes to Healing: Mystical Encounters with the Holocaust,* which is about people who died in the Holocaust but have currently reincarnated. In his letter to me, he said that he'd read my book and noticed that I wrote about my intense disdain for my friend's shiny black boots. He stated that in his research, he'd discovered that there are many similarities among people who are alive now but had perished during the Holocaust. One of those things was the unanimous dislike of shiny black boots.)

As this woman described her childhood love of Hitler's manifesto, I began to understand the underlying dynamics of our relationship. I had first met her in New Zealand after I'd injured myself from a fall down a cliff side. Although we barely knew each other, for the weeks that I was on my back with a damaged spine, she brought me food and took care of me. I could now see that this was a reenactment of our life together in Auschwitz—as a prison guard, she felt compassion for the prisoners and tried to minister to them. I also understood why I'd so strongly disliked her black boots. Although she was kind to me in the camp, her boots reminded me of all the Nazi officials.

At the time I called a dear family friend who had done extensive regression work and—on a hunch—asked him about any connection he might have had with Nazi Germany. He said that he was currently reading a book about the Holocaust, and he definitely remembered having been in a concentration camp in a past life. In fact, the very night that I'd called he was planning a pilgrimage to Auschwitz because he felt he had some unfinished business there. I asked if there was anything in his childhood to give credence to the fact that he'd been a prisoner in a concentration camp. He replied that when he was a boy, although he was a Christian, he'd asked his mother for a Star of David pendant. He even remembered his response when people would ask why he wore it: It was so he'd never forget the crimes against humanity that had been perpetrated.

My friend also mentioned some unusual events that had occurred when he'd visited Germany in his present life: The instant he crossed the border, his watch stopped, his electric razor wouldn't work, and he developed a rash. When he left the country, his watch and shaver started working once again and his rash disappeared. Currently, he's a volunteer counselor for prisoners. He said he often feels that the inmates he works with were the Nazi prison wardens in his past life at Auschwitz. He feels that his prison work is helping to heal old emotional wounds.

At different times in our lives, previous incarnations and their associated issues become prevalent. At that time I must have been ready to begin to deal with my life in a concentration camp, which is why it was finally emerging. Shortly after that experience, I was asked to teach in Germany. Although I'd traveled fairly extensively throughout the world, it was the only country I'd ever visited where attendance at my lectures was limited and I didn't enjoy myself. Yet for some reason I returned again and again, as if deep inside me there was a yearning to forgive the past . . . a past that I couldn't quite bring myself to remember.

When I finally decided not to return to Germany, the promoters told me that I spoke to them in perfect German when I explained that I wasn't coming back. This shocked them—and stunned me—because I thought I was speaking English. In that moment, my past life must have filtered through to the present time. Perhaps there's much more of the puzzle for me to unfold. I still don't have any visual images or memories, but I know that the issues from that traumatic lifetime are healed for the most part. I've just started teaching in Germany again after a hiatus of many years, and remarkably, all I feel now is joy and enthusiasm while there. I love the people I encounter and always have wonderful experiences. (The journey into my past lives that began with my childhood dreams has now come full circle!)

In the coming years, you may find an increase in the past-life images that appear in your dreams; therefore, it's important to remember them so that these images don't sift gently back into your subconscious.

Remembering Your Dreams

Science has proven that everyone dreams. Even those who swear that they don't dream, in fact, do so—it's just that they don't remember their dreams, as the majority stay in our consciousness for only ten minutes. For this reason, it's valuable to keep a notebook or tape recorder next to your bed so that you can quickly record your dreams before they fade from memory. Researchers have shown that dreams occur when people are in a very light sleep state toward the end of a sleep cycle (a cycle lasts 90 minutes). Therefore, you won't feel tired later by taking some time to write down your dreams because you'll be waking up at the normal conclusion of a sleep cycle. Using a small flashlight kept beside your bed, rather than turning on the bedroom light, will enable you to fall sleep more easily after noting the content of your dreams.

Remembering your dreams is like any other skill. As you practice, you'll increase your ability to remember. You might want to note the date and time of your dreams to see if a pattern begins to emerge.

On the next page is an exercise that you can do just before sleep to help you remember your dreams.

Programming Your Dreams

As you lie down to go to sleep, take a moment to relax completely. You might begin by slowing your breath. Take long, deep breaths. Inhale fully and exhale completely.

As you begin to relax, tell yourself, "All thoughts and cares are drifting away." Imagine that you're standing beside a slow-moving river. Visualize picking up your cares one by one and placing them in the river in the kind of leaf-and-stick boats that children make. Watch each one gently float away, taking with it each and every concern. This clears your mind of interference, and you can relax even more.

Next, starting with your toes, go through your body, allowing each part to let go. For example, focus upon your right foot; breathe deeply, holding the breath for a second; and then exhale, allowing your right foot to become totally limp and free of tension. Continue until your entire body is utterly at ease. Some people report feeling so heavy that they couldn't move if they wanted to; others say that it feels like floating on a cloud.

Once you're completely relaxed, make sure that your spine is straight. Then imagine a blue light at the back of your throat, and say aloud to yourself (as the spoken word often has greater impact on the subconscious mind): "Tonight I travel to one of my past lives . . . and I remember my dreams." Hold this in mind with as much intensity as you can as you drift off to sleep.

The visualization of a blue light in the throat is an ancient Tibetan technique—although, interestingly, its basis may lie in scientific fact. Modern research has shown that dreams originate in the brain stem, which lies directly behind the back of the throat. Studies have also supported the notion that focusing attention on one part of the anatomy increases the blood circulation to that area. So putting your attention on the back of your throat can increase the blood flow to the brain stem and thus cause a heightened awareness while dreaming.

When programming your dreams, try to concentrate on one particular area of your life that needs assistance, and focus on that just before you fall asleep. As you're practicing the blue-light technique, concentrate on the *feeling* associated with the area that you want to work on in your dreams. Here are some subjects that you might want to bring your attention to just before sleep.

Programming Dreams to
Release Phobias and Fears

Fears and phobias often have their source in a past life. Are you so afraid of confronting your boss that your work life is nearly unbearable? Are you constantly anxious about your health? As you fall asleep, use the blue-light technique and at the same time think about the fear you want to resolve. Take a moment to focus on the physical effects that this problem creates in your body. Are you breathing quickly, does your stomach feel tight, is your throat constricted, or do you have a headache? Be aware of physical sensations that accompany your thoughts about the issue. Then imagine that the energy of the blue light is pervading the part (or parts) of your body where the most tension is accumulated. Say aloud to yourself, "Dreams, show me the source of my fear in a past life, and lead me to a resolution of it." Continue to focus your attention at the back of your throat as you feel the blue-light energy gently infusing your whole body as you drift off to sleep.

Programming Dreams to
Release Physical Ailments and Injuries

Sometimes our current physical challenges are symbolic of past-life traumas. For example, a man who has breathing problems may have had a past life in which he suffocated to death. And a woman with chronic back pain may have had a life in which she felt that she could never stand up for herself.

As I described in the previous section, place your awareness on the area of your body that's troubling you. If you have many physical problems and the feelings are overwhelming, choose the most intense one.

Stay with the feeling for a moment, and then imagine the blue light gently entering that part of your body, bringing healing and relief. Say to yourself, *Dreams, reveal to me the source of my discomfort and ailments so that it can be healed. Take me back to the time when I first experienced this problem.* Hold this thought in the back of your throat amid the blue light, and gently go to sleep.

Programming Dreams to
Release Relationship Difficulties

The people you're very close to, as well as those whom you have great difficulty with, are likely to have been important to you in earlier lifetimes. (For more information, you can review the section on soul mates in Chapter 2.) Remembering the dynamics of relationships in previous incarnations—and seeing how they affect the way you relate to people in this life—can help you explore completely different ways of being with others. To program your dreams for recollection of these issues, follow the steps described earlier for overcoming fears and physical ailments. Allow yourself to experience the bodily sensations associated with your difficult relationships. When you're not getting along with someone close to you, what part of your body is most affected? Focus on that area and tell yourself, *My dreams will allow me to remember the significance of this relationship in another lifetime, and they'll lead me to a wonderful and fulfilling resolution of this issue in my life now.*

Programming Dreams to
Release Blockages to Abundance

Many people create a climate of deprivation for themselves out of a sense of guilt or a feeling that they don't deserve good things. Oftentimes, these beliefs seem to have no relation to the circumstances of a person's current life. Perhaps you're living in the best manner you can and have no conscious awareness of any nagging guilt, but you just can't get over the feeling that you don't deserve to have the things you want. Feeling this way leads to a continual state of poverty consciousness, which prevents you from manifesting abundance in all aspects. Going into the past and locating the source of your feelings of unworthiness can free you from this cycle of lack and deprivation. In addition to programming your dreams to release the original past-life blockages, try the following exercise.

Instead of concentrating on the feelings associated with your difficulty, focus on the desired results. For example, if you're having money problems, imagine the feelings you'd have if you were financially secure. As you lie in bed, form a clear picture of the material things you'd like to possess, where you'd like to travel, and whatever circumstances would allow you to enjoy your life more fully. Relax and let your mind play with these pictures. Enjoy the sights, sounds, and smells associated with the things you desire. Then say to yourself, *Tonight when I'm sleeping, I'll remember where and when I first came to believe that I couldn't have all that I desire and deserve. Tonight, my dreams will help me resolve my problems concerning money.*

Let this resolve be filled with the pleasure of all the wonderful things you've just envisioned. Push away any fear and anxiety about what you feel is currently lacking. Let yourself slip off to sleep, secure in the knowledge that these issues will be settled and that the things you wish for are already in the process of becoming part of your reality. Hold your intention lightly and joyously in the back of your throat as you do the blue-light exercise.

Writing Down Your Dreams

As soon as you wake up, *immediately* write down what you remember even if it seems insignificant. When you first begin to enter the past while dreaming, you might find just a hint of something that appears to be from a previous incarnation. Past-life fragments get woven into dreams that seem to be concerned purely with present-life issues. For example, you might dream that you're zooming down a freeway in a red sports car, but as you look out your window, you see someone dressed in 17th-century garb. It's as if there's a semipermeable membrane between this life and past ones.

At first, just an object or two from a past life will make it through the membrane into your dream world. As you become more skilled with your dream states, inner dimensional portals will be made available so that parts or whole scenes will seep through into the present dimension. Eventually, you'll be able to step through a time-traveler's portal, enabling you to be completely immersed in a past life. Until that time, be sure to jot down everything you dream about. I believe that even the most ordinary dreams have past-life clues hidden within them.

Analyzing Your Dreams

See if there's any similarity between your past-life dreams and your current life. Is there someone from a previous lifetime who strikes you as very similar to someone you know now? Notice your emotions in that past life and any decisions or judgments you made. Are any patterns, habits, or fears in that life present now? For example, let's say you dream of being lost in a snowstorm and are frightened, and in your current life you always avoid being outside during harsh weather. This dream could be evidence of your past-life trauma. But remember, *one clue isn't enough.* You must become a "reincarnation detective" and put all the clues together to form a clear picture.

For example, I recently had a dream that I was in a building with small rooms. Many people were crowded inside, and there was a pervading feeling of fear. The major themes were small rooms, crowding, and not feeling safe. I listed these important aspects of the dream, and the next step was to look for some correlation to my present life.

At that time we were remodeling our home, and the contents of a number of rooms were packed into just a few. It felt very crowded. In addition, due to the construction work, some of the doors were off their hinges—perhaps subconsciously I felt that our home wasn't safe. This seemed like a reasonable explanation for my dream. Then I saw the film *Schindler's List,* and I was astonished to see that the crowded rooms I'd dreamed of only nights before looked almost exactly like the rooms in the Warsaw ghetto where many Jews were crowded into before they were rounded up and sent to concentration camps. My dream had a correlation with my present life, but at the same time it provided another clue for me as I continued to explore the life during which I was interned in Auschwitz.

For some people, past lives appear visually and specifically in their dreams, while others wake up with no visual images but have a profound feeling or sensation.

If you've programmed your dreams as I described and you awaken with no specific mental pictures, take a moment to notice what you're feeling. If you feel sad, expand the sadness into a story. It might go like this: "This sadness feels like the kind that a person would experience if they lost someone very close to them— perhaps a child. It doesn't feel like my child but someone else's. The little one was carefree and happy, and I wish I could have warned this joyful being not to get too close to the waterfall." When you make up your story, don't be overly concerned if it's right. The more you struggle to be *correct,* the more difficult it is for the images to flow from your subconscious.

Write down your stories as well as the memories of your dreams. Sometimes the stories will seem to have a life of their own and take shape without any effort. It's very important, however, to do this exercise just as you're waking up. This is the most powerful time for your subconscious to give you information about your past. Often people tell me that when they review their journal entries and dream memories, they've been able to watch as the pieces of their reincarnation puzzle begin to fall into place.

Dream Sequencing and Interpretation

Another technique for understanding a past-life connection in your dreams is to continue the experience once you're awake. I call this *dream sequencing.* To start, set aside 20 to 30 minutes during any time of the day. Find a comfortable chair or bed, and make sure you won't be disturbed. Take a few minutes to relax completely. You can either deepen your breathing or visualize a pleasant scene. Once you're relaxed, let your mind go back into the dream from the preceding night. Even if you recall just a wisp of it, the exercise will still work. Now replay what you can remember, allowing the images to evolve on their own. Don't consciously try to direct the outcome of the scene that's unfolding. Let your imagination roam freely, as a sequence is forming from the fragment of your dream.

Don't be concerned if some of the things occurring don't seem to make sense, such as glimpsing a 16th-century queen wearing a crown made of Tupperware. Remember that the language of dreams is symbolic. Your sleeping mind is like an artist weaving together a rich tapestry of images—mixing a bit of this with a bit of that. This is the way it communicates. In order to understand, you have to let go of your need for everything to fit together in a logical way. Just try to get the *feel* of what the images evoke for you.

Continue allowing the dream sequence to unfold. If at any time you encounter something uncomfortable, surround yourself in an imaginary bubble of safety or change the series of events so that the situation resolves itself.

Oftentimes while you're dreaming, people, things, and places have symbolic significance. This is as true for past-life dreams as for those that are connected mostly with our present life. Carl Jung and other researchers studied the many universal symbols that people all over the world recognize and employ in their art and religion and that also show up in their dreams; these are called *archetypes.* If you recognize someone famous in your dream sequence, you might of course have known him or her in another life, but more often the well-known figure is an archetypal symbol. If Geronimo appears in your dreams, it's likely that he represents the part of you that's "strength against all odds."

It can be a challenging task to distinguish which dreams are related to your present life and which are clearly from the past. Additionally, individuals and things may appear in dreams literally (as themselves and not representative of something else), while other times they act as symbols for something or someone else. I think the important thing is to trust your instincts. *Your feelings are your best guide to interpreting your dreams.* Does the antique chest, which looks just like your grandmother's, feel as if it has something to do with your present family, or does your heart lead you in an entirely different direction?

When you've completed your dream sequence, write it down in your journal—be sure to add it to the clues that you're accumulating.

Dream Meditation Process

This meditation process, based on ancient dream techniques, is safe and easy and should be done just before sleep. It's best to record this meditation and play it back to yourself right after you settle into bed. Speak in a slow, relaxed voice. If you like, you can substitute "I" for "you" in the meditation. You might want to include some background music, too. (Remember to always keep your dream journal next to your bed so you can easily keep track of your dreams.)

Allow your body to assume a restful position, making sure that your spine is straight. You may do this now. Good.

Now begin to take very easy, deep breaths. Inhale and exhale. That's good. It's as if nothing else exists except for your breath. All your thoughts and cares are drifting away as you continue to breathe in and out. With each breath, you feel more relaxed. You find yourself moving deeper and deeper within yourself. Imagine that you're flowing into your body as you inhale . . . and out of your body as you exhale. It's as if you're drifting with the very gentle ebb and flow of the universe, and your breath is connecting you to that rhythm. Breathe gently and evenly as you continue your journey into a very relaxed, yet aware, state.

Feel any tightness just dissolving like ice melting on a warm summer afternoon. That's good. Imagine in your mind's eye, a moonlit night. There's a beautiful full moon, and you're walking along the sandy seashore. Glowing in the moonlight ahead is a bed—it's luxurious and voluptuous. The pillows are soft and round. Take some time to imagine this, making it as real as possible. Visualize your perfect sleeping place.

Now, slowly and ever so sensuously, crawl into this bed. Be aware of the opulent plumpness of the pillows and the silky smoothness of the sheets as you slide easily between them. It feels so good to be here. Comforted by the gentle sounds and cadence of the sea as the tides ebb and flow, you find yourself lulled into a deep sleep.

Somewhere in the magic of the night, a metamorphosis will occur. You know that you'll be delicately transported back to another place . . . another time. You'll be guided to one of your previous lives. You're aware of a door to the past that will make itself evident in your dreams. As your body sleeps, your spirit will travel through time and space, dancing through the stars and touching past incarnations.

Now imagine that you're going forward in time, to the moment when you're about to wake up. Your dreams are still very evident. Picture yourself rolling over in bed and writing down those dreams—images that hold the keys to your past lives.

You may now either return to conscious awareness or drift off to sleep.

You can repeat this meditation again and again. I wish you well on your inner journeys.

Chapter Eight

RESOLUTION: HOW TO HEAL PAST-LIFE BLOCKAGES DURING REGRESSION

One of the main benefits of regression therapy is that it can finally free you of the hindrances that have been holding you back throughout many lifetimes. However, for this to occur you need to learn how to resolve those blockages. This chapter contains a number of simple exercises you can do alone or with a friend to finally unravel the lingering issues that have been obstructing your life. (I suggest that you try several or all of the exercises to find out which ones work best for you.)

Resolution Method One: Choose It

People have often asked me, "What if I do the processes and come up with a lifetime that's scary . . . or what if I have a past-life nightmare?" Instead of shutting down or suppressing these emotions, *choose* to feel them—when you do so, the fear will dissipate. For example, when you see an action thriller at the movie theater, you pay to be frightened; you're going out of your way to create an intense experience for yourself. When you hop on a roller-coaster ride and are absolutely terrified, remember that it was *you* who rushed to join the line. There are times in life when we choose to be scared, but we're not overwhelmed *because it was by choice.*

Don't be afraid of the emotions you might encounter when you get in touch with a past life. *Choose them.* No one would attend an orchestral performance if only one note was to be played. A symphony needs thousands of tones—high points and low. Life is like that, too. Enjoy all your emotions and think of each one as a precious note in your unique musical composition. As you experience a past life, relish and explore each feeling that arises.

If you find yourself stuck in an emotion during a past-life journey, don't deny it or try to get rid of it; instead, move toward it and choose it. See yourself confronting that feeling and letting it flow all around you. Exaggerate it. For instance, if you discover a lifetime in which you were devastated by the death of your lover, instead of trying to deny or repress the grief—which is what you did at the time—let yourself feel even sadder.

Go to the center of that sorrow. Find the spot in your body where it resides, and allow yourself to enter into it. This will enable you to begin releasing the issues that have been creating barriers for you.

Don't Dramatize It—Experience It

What you resist persists. When you resist an emotion, it actually becomes more difficult to release it. What you repress stays with you lifetime after lifetime and creates blockages, so it's vital to face your feelings. However, there's a difference between *dramatizing* and *experiencing* them.

When I began conducting past-life therapy seminars, many people would cry or sob during the processes— sometimes very dramatically. I assumed this was an important step toward the ultimately positive results they would achieve. Then when I led a seminar in Vancouver, Canada, and nobody cried uncontrollably, I was distraught, thinking my techniques hadn't worked. However, I was astonished to receive numerous letters afterward from participants of that seminar claiming positive results. I figured it was a fluke, but the same thing occurred in my next seminar and has continued ever since.

In my past-life seminars today, almost no one becomes emotional even though very dramatic, positive results are always reported. As I began to investigate this phenomenon, I realized that instead of externalizing and amplifying their emotions, people were going to the source of their feelings . . . and truly embracing them. As strange as it sounds, sometimes dramatizing your emotions can actually keep you separate from them.

I met a woman who'd been crying almost every day for 20 years over the death of her husband; despite how much she cried, she couldn't overcome her grief. Her sadness never dissipated. When she went inside her body to the source of it, she was finally able to truly grieve for the first time in all those years. She then "experienced" her anguish instead of externalizing it and was able to release it completely. By finding the place in your body where the emotion exists and going into it, you can release it at its roots.

To Heal It, Embrace It

This is an exercise you can do if you begin to feel any uncomfortable emotions during your past-life regressions. It's similar, in some ways, to the "Body Wisdom" method that I discussed in an earlier chapter in which you experience an emotion as a physical sensation in order to find a past life. However, the focus for this exercise is on *resolution* of a past-life difficulty.

As I just mentioned, if you encounter a previous incarnation in which you discover a very difficult event or face some challenging emotions, begin by traveling throughout your body to locate the feeling associated with the traumatic event. (There's always a sensation in your body that's associated with an emotion.) For example, your chest might feel constricted during sadness and your shoulders might tighten during anger. However, not everyone experiences emotions in the same way.

Once you've located the emotion you're feeling, focus your entire attention on that part of your body and *intensify* the sensation. If you feel a constriction in your chest, make it tighter. *Feel it more.* As you do so, identify what shape the emotion/sensation seems to be.

The tightness in the chest associated with sadness might seem pear shaped, with the smaller end of the pear pointing downward. As you focus on the area, also observe how large the sensation is. The pear might seem about six inches wide and eight inches long. Then notice if it has a color. (It's not mere coincidence that people associate particular colors with certain emotions: "She's in the pink," "He's feeling blue," "I'm having a black day," "He saw red," and so on.)

Continue to ask yourself these questions:

- *If there was a place in my body associated with this emotion, where might it be?* (Sometimes the sensation will shift to various spots in the body. Follow it wherever it goes).

- *If the sensation had a shape, what would it look like?*

- *If the sensation had a size, how big would it be?*

- *If the sensation had a color, what color would it be?*

Keep on intensifying what you're feeling. Often the color, shape, size, and location change as you're doing this exercise, but continue moving into your emotions, rather than away from them. Just practicing these steps is usually enough to begin releasing the uncomfortable feelings that arose during your past-life experiences. What you resist persists . . . and when you quit resisting what you're feeling, it can dissolve.

Sometimes when you do this exercise, memories from another past life will emerge spontaneously. In the same way that a temper tantrum thrown at age 20 may be the result of a temper tantrum thrown under similar circumstances at age 3, so the past-life trauma that you're working with may have its source in even another, similar lifetime. So don't be surprised if you find yourself catapulted from one former incarnation to another. It's beneficial because with each time jump you're getting even closer to the source of your present-life difficulty. Doing this exercise can allow the undesirable emotions and the past-life blockage to disappear.

Resolution Method Two: Detach from It

If you find yourself in a past-life memory that holds very uncomfortable emotions, imagine that you're floating above the scene and just observe it. Let go of the particular view that you held at the time.

When you detach from a situation, you can observe it from a greater, more objective perspective. Beryl experienced a lifetime in which her husband died of an infection he contracted while working in their garden. In her regression, she felt tremendous sadness tinged with guilt over her loss. The sadness was for the loss of her husband; the guilt was due to the fact that she'd been capable of completing the garden work but told her husband that she wasn't strong enough to do it. Although of course it wasn't her fault, she felt culpable, and that emotion had permeated her present life.

When she detached from the scene and floated above it to gain an expanded perspective, she saw that her intense love for her husband was sometimes to the detriment of her children. She often put aside their needs in order to spend more time with her spouse. After his death, she began to nurture her kids more and give them the attention and love they needed. When she removed herself from the picture, she was able to come to terms with her husband's death and understand that everything has a purpose, even if she didn't realize it at the time.

When you detach from a scene, you can float above it or watch it as if you were viewing a movie. If it's very traumatic, you can observe yourself looking at the scene as a way of further detaching from the situation.

Another technique I often suggest is to fast-forward the incident at high speed, like an old Charlie Chaplin film. Then run it backward at high speed. For example, if you find yourself running and falling off a cliff, see yourself running and falling very fast and then flipping up off the ground, soaring back to the top of the cliff, and running backward! This exercise, which can make any seemingly distressful event humorous, can help you detach from it.

Yet another way to remove yourself from an uncomfortable past life is to make it seem silly. A client who had always felt intimidated by men came to me for help. She was a mature, responsible woman but as soon as she was near a man, she began to act in a meek, childlike way. Having regressed to a life in which she had a strict, disciplinarian father, she saw that whenever she was with men, she activated the memory of being a timid little girl from that past life. During her regression, she arrived at a point where her father was giving her a stern dressing-down. I told her to imagine him standing in front of her wearing red spotted pants and a silly hat as people walked by and laughed. Suddenly she, too, was laughing, and she was no longer a submissive young girl. This session completely changed her attitude toward men.

Detaching from a past-life scene helps you understand that every lifetime you have allows you to grow—and that everything you encounter is important for your evolution as a soul. When you observe a past life with an objective point of view, you see that Spirit is interested not so much in your comfort as in your personal growth, even if it means going through difficult, painful experiences.

Resolution Method Three: Change It

The most powerful technique to resolve an uncomfortable past-life issue is to change the circumstances of that life until it feels comfortable or enjoyable. I believe that you can actually change the past. If this is too far-fetched for you to accept, then imagine that you're altering the images stored in your brain. As you transform them, you also change the associated limiting beliefs.

I believe that the future and the past are malleable, and from the viewpoint of physics, this isn't a totally far-fetched idea. According to scientists, time is a function of gravity and it can shorten or lengthen depending on how far away you are from the gravitational pull of the earth. I don't know whether this scientific fact applies to the metaphysical notion that time is an illusion, but it does give credence to the idea that time isn't as we usually perceive it.

Personally, I've experienced profound changes in my own life—and in the lives of others—simply by going into past lives and altering the events. Whether you believe, as I do, that you're actually altering your past or if you're just *imagining* that the past is different isn't important. What *is* important is that as a result of these changes, your life transforms in positive and powerful ways.

There are many cases of individuals regressing to a past life and healing the wounds that occurred at the time (and continue to play out in their present life) simply by changing the memories they'd associated with that event (or by changing the meaning they gave to it). That past-life healing then transforms their present-day lives. In other words, when you heal your past—by changing those past events—you can create a balanced and harmonious future.

Past-life therapy works in an extraordinary way. When you go back and release the negative beliefs locked up in previous lifetimes, you can profoundly alter the history of your existence right from the beginning. This may sound unbelievable, but I've witnessed case after case where individuals in my seminars literally went to the past, changed it, and came back to an altered present. The changes weave themselves through time, creating a new future. I believe that this is a phenomenon whose time has come, and you'll find it appearing more and more often in films and books.

Changing the memories of a previous incarnation and, as a consequence, creating a better outcome for yourself is the most compelling method for resolution that I know of. When you re-create your past, you no longer need to view yourself as a victim—you can take control of your life. And you always have the power to create an empowering past! Accept the soul growth that each life offers and at the same time, create a past that supports you and gives you joy. On a soul level, each lifetime was perfect for your evolution, but at the same time, former experiences don't need to repeat in your future. It's never too late to have a blissful past. However, if it seems too philosophical to think about really changing old events, just consider it as altering the past that dwells within your mind. All the memories—and all the associated limiting beliefs and negative programming—exist in your mind. *Change your mind and change your life.*

Whether you believe that you're actually manipulating the past or that you're just modifying your own memories, it doesn't matter—it really works!

Remember the earlier example of Joshua, the young man whose friends chased him into a ravine when they thought he was ridiculing the king? Imagine that he changes this past-life memory. He stops running and stands his ground, and those who were chasing him stop. He proceeds to tell everyone what he thinks. There's a standoff . . . then everyone bursts out laughing. Changing his mental picture from being physically and emotionally hurt to a vision of speaking his mind transforms the previous inner belief that he'd developed. When his limiting belief changes, his life changes. A man who fears that he'll be punished if he speaks the truth will create circumstances to validate his subconscious belief. Physical matter coalesces around us based on our subconscious beliefs. *Change your subconscious beliefs and the world around you will seem to change, too.*

The following letter, sent to me after a past-life seminar, shows the power of recasting your past-life memories.

I would like to share with you, Denise, a past life that I became aware of during your weekend past-life workshop, which has had an enormous impact on my life now. In my present life, my son was born with the umbilical cord around his neck and has always been a screamer. He also had a speech pattern where he'd repeat several words in the sentence many times. He is now a three-and-a-half-year-old, and an example of his type of speech is as follows: "The cat, cat, cat, cat is running, running very, very, very, very fast, fast."

The past life I experienced in your Journeys into Past Lives seminar was a life where my son and I both were American Indians. I was my current son's mother and he was about 11 years old. My son and I were separated from our tribe and another tribe attacked us. In the past-life regression, I was facing several of the attackers. It became clear to me that they were going to kill me and torture my son. I became very angry and tried to convince them to leave my son alone. When it was obvious that this wasn't working, I turned to my son and we both looked deeply into each other's eyes. My son, in an instant, understood what I was going to do: We both screamed and I strangled him.

I don't know why, but I survived the attack and lived the rest of my lifetime with the anguish of having killed my own son. During the regression, I changed the outcome (as you suggested). I saw many images of beautiful crystals; total safety; and wonderful, open, clear communication between my son and myself. For me, this was very exciting.

It became even more exciting when, after the seminar, I returned to pick up my son from my mother's and she proceeded to tell me that at one point during the weekend my son had gone into the bedroom and began to sob and sob. The sobbing continued for nearly 30 minutes . . . he couldn't seem to stop. This happened at the exact same time as I was getting in touch with our life together as Indians.

I am writing this just one week later and my son has completely stopped the word repetitions in his sentences, and his screaming has also subsided. I used to be so wound up by his screaming that I wanted to put my hands around his neck. Although I never did, the urge to do so was very strong—almost overwhelming.

This regression has been a major turning point for us. I feel really excited and empowered as a result of the weekend. Thank you for a most special experience.

By changing the circumstances of a past life that this woman and her son were reliving, not only did she change the way she felt about her son, but she changed his behavior as well! In a very curious turn of events, an almost exact scenario unfolded in another past-life seminar. A little boy who previously didn't speak began to talk during the exact time of his mother's regression, as she changed the life that she was experiencing even though her son was miles away!

Here's another letter I received that shows the value of altering the circumstances of a traumatic past life.

I was one of the several hundred people at your Past Life Seminar in Sydney in November. You may remember me as the woman who gave you a book during the seminar. My reason for writing is to tell you about the incredible occurrences that have happened over the last few days since your seminar.

When my husband and his first wife divorced 11 years ago, it was very bitter and he was stopped from seeing his children—in particular the youngest child, who was seven years old at the time. My husband is a special person and this has been hard on him.

During one of the weekend's regressions, I concentrated on the thought that if I'd been a part of my husband's family in a past life, I wanted some insight and understanding. Well, I'm still not sure exactly what my role was in the past life that I experienced, except that I saw that I was comforting an old man who was dying. He wasn't dying of old age but of a broken heart, blaming himself for the deaths by drowning of his three children. I recognized that the old man was my present-day husband.

You told us that we could change what was upsetting, so I changed the situation. It was in the future in that life and I was dying, and the old man and his three children were comforting me. They were very close and happy. This apparently had an effect on the present! Today the youngest child, seemingly out of the clear blue, called and is coming to visit tomorrow. This is the most hopeful thing to have occurred in 11 years! Last night I told my husband about the regression and although he is skeptical, he is open-minded. Wow! So thank you, Denise. Isn't life grand when you know that love is all that matters!

This example shows that even if you aren't aware of all the details of your past life, just changing the circumstances can have an empowering effect on your present life.

Here's a personal example from my life that shows the step-by-step mechanics of how to recast past-life memories.

When my daughter, Meadow, was younger, I asked her if I could try a new relaxation technique on her before I practiced it on my clients. I needed to hold her wrist, but as I did so, she said, "Mom, you know I don't like to have my wrists touched. In fact, I can't even look at my wrists because when I see the veins I get squeamish."

I hadn't been aware of this before but proceeded with the relaxation process. Once she was relaxed, I thought I'd take the opportunity to see if I could get to the source of her difficulty.

I said, "Imagine a situation that might relate to your wrists." (Children, incidentally, can usually regress very easily into past lives, but adults often develop a buffer to their intuition, making it more difficult to be regressed. However, I don't suggest regressing any children until they are of consenting age.)

"Mom, I see a desert. I live in the desert."

"Are you male or female?"

"I'm a young man. I have a religious belief that I feel strongly about. It's a good belief, and I want to tell everyone about it because I know it will help them. I'm now in a small village preparing to talk to people about this new belief. They don't want to know about it—in fact, they're getting very angry. Oh no!"

"What is it?"

"They're tying me up. They've cut my wrists . . . I'm watching the blood slowly flow out of my body. I'm tied up so I can't stop it. I'm dying!"

"You can change this experience," I told her calmly. "You can replay it but give it a positive outcome."

"Okay. I'm replaying it . . . I've traveled across the desert to tell the villagers about my new religion. Everyone who greets me is happy to meet me and seems really interested in talking and finding out about my beliefs. When I leave the village, I've made many good friends."

"How do you feel?"

"I feel great. It feels good to know that I can really tell people how I feel."

All this occurred in about 20 minutes. My daughter came back from her experience feeling refreshed and rejuvenated. I asked her to look at the veins on her wrists, and she was amazed that she could now look at them without feeling queasy.

Up until that point, she'd always been hesitant to say how she truly felt about anything. In fact, she was probably the least opinionated person I had ever known. But now a remarkable thing occurred. It was hard to believe it was the same child. Meadow began to tell people how she felt about things and to share her personal points of view. This was something that she'd never done before! The Gulf War broke out soon afterward, and Meadow called all the students in her class and asked them to march against the war with her. Some students agreed with her while others vehemently disagreed. She felt strongly about the war and was willing to let other people know her true beliefs. To me, this was a minor miracle. I believe that our one 20-minute session made all the difference.

Some people are concerned that if they change the past, they'll negatively affect the present. They'll ask, "What if I change the past and then my mother never meets my father. Will I still exist?" Such questions are interesting to me, philosophically, but in my experience, changing a traumatic past life always has a positive effect on everyone. When you clear an emotional blockage from your energy field, you create a resonance that deeply impacts you and others for the best. You *can* change the past. Just shifting the images in your brain associated with limiting beliefs has a beneficial and empowering effect on life.

Resolution Method Four:
See It from Another Viewpoint

A technique for resolving past-life situations that involve another person is to imagine that you're jumping into the awareness or the body of that individual. See the entire situation from his or her point of view. When you do so, you almost always forgive the other's actions because you recognize that you would have reacted in the same way.

Although I definitely don't condone the actions of the man who shot me, it was enormously helpful for me to imagine that I was in his consciousness. When I did that, I felt that he couldn't stop himself from killing people, in much the same way that addicts can't control their cravings. Seeing life through his eyes made it much easier for me to forgive him. This was valuable for me because resentment could have arisen later.

Another interesting example is the case of Charlotte. She'd been quarreling with her younger sister seemingly since her sister was born. The fighting had continued into adulthood, and their arguments were having a negative effect on the entire family, as they tried to get other family members to agree with their points of view. Charlotte became aware that these altercations were becoming increasingly counterproductive and affecting many areas of her life.

She attended a past-life workshop I gave in New Zealand and recalled a life in which she was an accounting clerk in Denmark, and her present-life sister was her demanding and argumentative employer. In the regression, she took my suggestion of seeing the world through her employer's eyes. Instantly, she understood that her employer had very severe back pain that made his every move painful. Because of his debilitating pain, he was continually in a foul mood and treated his employees badly.

With this new understanding, Charlotte began to feel compassion for her employer/sister. (It's interesting to note that her sister in her present life also had a back injury.) Charlotte reported that she saw her sister a few days after the seminar and was astonished to find that there was much less animosity between them. Their relationship has continued to grow closer.

Resolving past-life blockages is one of the most rewarding kinds of work you can do. Many of my clients have reported a greater sense of exhilaration and joy than they'd ever experienced before . . . but it can be a rough and rocky road while you're in the process. Share your challenges with someone who cares about you, or seek professional assistance if you think you need it, and know that what awaits you is more than worth it.

Chapter Nine

Spirit Guides, Angels, and Past Lives

During your past-life explorations, it's immensely valuable to call upon the assistance of spirit guardians. They can help you discover and heal your past lives, as well as make you feel safe while you embark on your regressions. The importance of asking for their guidance as you delve into your past can't be overestimated! This chapter will give you information about your spirit guides and how they can be of benefit to you in your life now and in your reincarnation journeys.

What Are Spirit Helpers?

Even if you don't believe in them, you *do* have spiritual guardians who deeply and profoundly love you. In fact, everyone has guides whether they're consciously aware of it or not . . . but not everyone knows how to listen to these ethereal mentors. However, when you take the time to consciously communicate with your spirit helpers, you gain admittance to an enormous wealth of resources, and they can also be powerful allies in your past-life explorations.

These nonphysical beings come from the world of Spirit and hold a unique perspective of the universe, creation, life, and eternal love. In addition to offering you assistance, they are a reminder of the realm beyond your present life and can help you release old karmic blockages.

You may have multiple spirit helpers and guides over a lifetime. They may enter for a short time during critical life passages or stay consistently for a long period. They each have their own personalities, goals, perspectives, and styles of communication—and may be with you during the quiet of meditation or arrive as an unseen, loving presence you feel around you as you go about your everyday activities. Guides may appear to you in a daydream or in a dream at night. They can also arrive as a physical feeling, smell, light, sound, or even just a sense of knowing that they are near.

Spirit guides are nonphysical beings who exist on higher planes of consciousness and work toward helping you further your evolution. They are usually—but not always—beings who've been with you in other lives and are now in the spirit world, providing assistance in your journey through life.

Some people view guides not as spiritual entities with a consciousness outside of themselves but as part of themselves. They feel that guides are a personification of their higher self and regard communicating with them as a way to activate intuition. They believe their guides are actually a part of themselves that they aren't normally in touch with. Psychologists usually share this view, explaining that guides are aspects of ourselves that we haven't yet "owned," acknowledged, or integrated into our personalities.

These two points of view aren't mutually exclusive. In the deepest sense, is there anything "out there" that isn't you? You are a part of all things. Your spiritual guardians are you, just as the sky, the sea, and the stars are you. I believe that each person in our lives, whether or not he or she has a physical body, represents an aspect of ourselves—that is, each person in my life is a part of me. Whatever the reality, many past-life therapists find it enormously valuable to work with guides and report that it's much easier to connect with previous incarnations if they first connect their patient to their spiritual helper. I've heard this view consistently from regression therapists around the world.

What Do Guides Do?

When you have a problem and a solution suddenly comes out of nowhere, that's often the mark of a guide's intervention. Moments of inspiration can be the result of a spirit guardian's assistance, too. Those times when you're down and then feel uplifted—again, for no apparent reason—may also indicate an intercession. Guides, angels, and spirit animals boost creativity, abundance, and healing; and they're able to harmonize difficult relationships, in addition to being your protector to help you avoid dangerous situations. They can assist you with cultivating personal qualities such as forgiveness, acceptance, and joy. Your spiritual advisers can even offer aid with mundane issues such as getting parking spaces, finding lost property, or choosing the right clothes to wear. *And they can help you connect with your past lives.*

In addition to assisting the past-life recall processes, one of the primary reasons for guide contact is to allow a deepening of the understanding that there are dimensions beyond our physical, earthly existence. They give a more expansive view surpassing our humanity and can be a source of spiritual inspiration.

Not so commonly known, however, is that in return for these gifts from the *other side,* we also offer a great deal to these guides. Just as we're evolving, so are our guides. They grow through working with us, sometimes throughout several lifetimes.

Trusting the Information from Guides

Traditional metaphysics holds the belief that if a spirit says something, it must be true. I don't agree with that. I believe that just because individuals die, they don't automatically become the sage on the mountaintop. If these beings were couch potatoes while they were alive, that won't change in death.

There are entities on the other side that are desperate to communicate and they'll chatter endlessly, regardless of whether their information is worthwhile or accurate. Some are no wiser or clearer than any of your acquaintances. For example, although you might value the opinion of your neighbor, you wouldn't necessarily drop everything and move to Tahiti if she told you to. When a guide gives you advice, it's all right to question it and even reject it. It's important to realize that guides, like friends, have opinions and personality quirks. These discarnate beings don't even necessarily agree with one another! If you compare the testimony of different guides channeled through mediums, you'll find that they rarely see eye to eye on issues.

Test any information against your own inner knowing. If it's useful, then take it as your own. If not, let it go. The important thing to remember is that you're making the choice—and ultimately, you're responsible for the outcome of all the decisions you make.

Guides, personal guardians, angels, and totems (also known as spirit or power animals) are wonderful sources of wisdom; however, it's easy to become too dependent on them and fall into the trap of asking their advice on every aspect of your life. As valuable as guides are, a vital part of your evolution is to be able to step beyond them and rely upon your own inner knowing. When you do this, you're connecting with your soul—that part of you that continues after the body is sloughed off.

Types of Spirit Helpers

There are many kinds of guides. Remember that like attracts like, so your guides will always reflect aspects of yourself—although this isn't always obvious. I know of one instance where a tough woman who taught self-defense was surprised to find that her guide was very soft and feminine. She was expecting a Viking or at least a samurai warrior. This woman eventually realized that her spirit helper offered balance in her life. In the same way, someone who is very disorganized or flamboyant may connect with a librarian-type being—again, to provide harmony.

Guides can also be angels. Although these heavenly ambassadors are excellent conveyors of universal love, they aren't always equipped to deal with earthly problems. Additionally, your guide may appear in the form of an animal. (I'll discuss angels and spirit animals in greater detail later in this chapter.) Moreover, people who come from cultures that honor the spirits of ancestors—such as in Africa or China—will often be presented with their ancestors as guides.

Remember that it's not the form the guide takes or the manner of communication that's important. The significance lies in the value the information has to you. Once you've established a relationship with your guides, you might notice a distinct feeling when they're nearby. Sometimes it's like a tingling sensation in a certain part of the body. For instance, Ann's little finger tingles when her spiritual mentor is present. Rachel's body will sway to and fro as a "yes" answer from her guide and side to side if her guide is saying no.

Some people hear their own name spoken or become aware of a distinctive odor or scent when their guide is close at hand. One man's spirit helper came from a past life in Eastern Europe—his presence was always accompanied by a distinct smell of sauerkraut. I get a tingling feeling between my shoulder blades when my master guide has something to say. Some people hear their guides speak, others get distinct visual images, and yet many just sense what their nonphysical mentor is trying to communicate. The important thing is to develop sensitivity so that you can be aware of and receive the messages from your spirit helpers.

Master Guide or Lifetime Guide

I've attended numerous births, and there's usually a point in which an influx of energy can be felt. This could be the influence of the birthing guides who are in attendance, but more often it represents the arrival of the master guide for the newborn baby. This is a being who will sometimes stay with you for an entire lifetime. Oftentimes your master guide has been present in a previous incarnation; however, if there's a change in life direction or emphasis, this being may step back and allow another master guide to come forward.

Many children report having an invisible friend. I believe that this unseen, imaginary companion is a spirit guardian, who assumes an identity that the child can communicate with as he or she develops. It's important to allow your kids to have that "friend" and not to discourage them or deny the existence of the relationship. Especially in early childhood, the master guide is there as an ally or as a kind of godparent, looking out for, protecting, and loving your child.

When I was very young, every night just before bed I was aware that someone else was also there with me. I never saw this individual, but I felt a wonderful, loving presence. This didn't seem unusual to me—it was as natural as breathing. As I got older, this warm presence visited me less and less. I believe those encounters were with my master guide, watching over me and protecting me during the night.

Special-Purpose Guides

Although some guides are lifelong companions, others come to help you in a particular area. For example, in my healing practice, a Native American guide assists me only while I'm actually working with an individual. I have another spirit helper who provides answers for my questions about diet. Artists and musicians very often have guides who boost creativity.

A special-purpose guide may enable you to develop a specific quality such as patience, perseverance, or abundance. I have a special guide who just helps me with my dreams—to program, remember, and understand them—and another one who assists with past-life awareness. There can even be specialty guides present during something as ordinary as shopping. I have a wonderful, voluptuous, redheaded shopping guide who wears dozens of dangling bracelets, dresses outrageously from head to foot, and speaks with a thick accent. When I'm at my wit's end and can't find what I need, she comes right in and—presto!—I find the perfect item.

Short-Term Guides

Sometimes a guide will arrive for just a short period. I was in New Mexico doing healing work with a man who had been in a traumatic automobile accident. As

I was about to begin, an old Native American woman guide came through and offered me unusual but specific information on how to treat my patient. I'd never seen this guide before and haven't seen her since, but I took her advice—and the results were excellent.

Later that day, I spent time with Dancing Feather and asked him about the advice I'd been given because it was so unfamiliar to me. He replied that the information I'd received was accurate according to the ways of the Pueblo Indians of that area. (Dancing Feather is now deceased, but he occasionally comes to me as a guide and often appears to those who attend my seminars.)

Sometimes these guides, such as the old Indian woman, only appear in a particular location . . . and are never seen again. I was attending a festival in a coastal village in Madeira, an island off the coast of Morocco. We were enjoying the warm evening as we strolled beneath the seawall. Suddenly a terrified shawl-clad woman appeared holding an unconscious child. The little one had fallen headfirst from the seawall and was now barely breathing, and the nearest doctor was hours away. The frightened mother looked to us for help and put her small son in my arms.

I was shocked and didn't know what to do, so I called for guide assistance. Instantly, I "saw" a spirit guardian who wore the old-fashioned vestments of a Catholic priest. He reached his arms out and placed them over the child. Suddenly the boy was conscious; he opened his eyes, and after a few minutes he was playing. The mother was immensely grateful, and I was also filled with gratitude for the spirit-guide intervention. Although I'd worked with ethereal guides for many years, the immediate power of this experience filled me with awe. I never saw this being again—apparently, he was indigenous to the area and remained there.

If you're interested in accessing your past lives, short-term guides may appear spontaneously or at your request to help you. They may also present themselves in your dreams or offer assistance during an emotionally or physically traumatic event in your life.

Guides from Your Past Lives

Sometimes guides are those whom you've shared a past life with. He or she may have taught you in the past, given you guidance, or been someone you loved deeply. These types of beings will often appear in a form that's familiar to you from the past experience you shared. For instance, if you had a life in a convent in the south of England in the 17th century, you might find that your spiritual mentor, who might have been the abbess during that lifetime, would dress accordingly—that's how she'd appear to you.

I became interested in past-life guides because of a phenomenon that occurred spontaneously again and again during regressions with my clients. Guardian figures would appear in these inner explorations, sometimes wearing clothing distinct to specific historical periods. In every instance, my clients would feel immediately soothed and comforted by the presence of these silent protectors.

Your inner journeys can allow guardian beings from past lives to surface. Not only do they spontaneously arise for people who are being regressed, but they can also appear in other types of meditations. People who've had near-death experiences often report that they were guided by protective spiritual entities that somehow seemed familiar to them. Meditators and even individuals who spend time in isolation tanks have witnessed guides and guardians who seemed to be from their past lives. Perhaps it's when we take the time to be still and turn our awareness inward that their presence can be felt most strongly.

Present-Life Guides

At times your guide will be someone you knew in your current life but who has died, such as a grandparent or another person whom you cared for as a child. This occurs frequently in my regression work with clients. There's an emotional connection between the individual and the guide that goes beyond time and space. Although the essence of the deceased stays the same, sometimes their personality changes when they're in the spirit world.

My Cherokee grandmother was very stoic and quiet when she was alive; she carried herself with the dignified demeanor of a Native American elder and was reserved with all her grandchildren. Although I respected her, she wasn't the kind of grandparent you wanted to cuddle with. I was therefore surprised when one day, many years after her death, she appeared in a dream to give me guidance. Gone was the stern gaze, and in its place was a wondrous, glowing Cherokee face filled with warmth and grace. I continue to feel her presence from time to time both in my dreams and in my waking life.

A guide can also be someone who's still alive. The very first time I attempted to contact a spirit guide in my meditation—almost 40 years ago—I saw a statuesque woman in her 50s who radiated magnificence. Two weeks later, I went for my first Rolfing session (Rolfing is a type of deep massage). When the door swung open, I was astonished to be greeted by the *exact* image of the woman from my meditation. It was the same person whom I'd seen; there was no doubt! Over the next few months, as Stacy Mills's sturdy fingers kneaded my muscles, this lovely woman healed my body and soul. At that time in my life, she was indeed a guide to me.

Although she wasn't consciously aware of it, her higher self was my spiritual mentor. With the exception of a guru, living guides don't usually realize the service that they're rendering. When you dream about someone you know in this lifetime helping you in some manner, that person's higher self is often actually assisting you. *You* might even be acting as a guide for others but aren't consciously aware of it.

Ancestors as Guides

In native and ancient cultures, ancestors weren't only honored but were also considered to be an enormous source of support and guidance for their descendants from their perspective in the spirit world. In Western culture, we no longer hold our forebearers in such high esteem; however, they can be a potent resource. Because of the bloodline connection, our ancestors can sometimes offer wisdom and assistance that is more meaningful than what we can gain from guides, totems, or angels.

Guides Aren't Ghosts

Guides are different from ghosts, as a ghost is basically someone who has died but hasn't fully realized or accepted it. A ghost is still on the Earth plane—but no longer has a body—and may be confused, sad, or angry. It's important to understand that they can't hurt you. When people have difficulty with these beings, they aren't harmed but are shaken by their own fears. Ghosts are at a great disadvantage because they no longer have a physical body. The kindest thing to do if you encounter one is to talk to him or her. Speak to the being as you would to anyone who is confused or unhappy, urging the soul to go to the Light. Be gentle but firm. (For more information about ghosts, please see my book *Sacred Space*.)

A Meditation for Finding Your Guide

The following meditation is designed to assist you in connecting with your guides. You can record it and play it back to yourself just before you go to sleep, or you can try it with a friend and ask him or her to read it aloud to you. (If you decide to record yourself reading the meditation, substitute *you* with *I*.)

You're about to embark on a voyage to the sacred place deep within yourself. Once you've tapped into this realm, you'll have access to a wellspring of wisdom, power, and peace. You're commencing a journey where you'll discover your sanctuary and encounter your guide. To prepare, lie down or sit in a comfortable position with your spine straight and your arms and legs uncrossed.

Do this now . . . good.

As soon as you're perfectly comfortable, allow your eyes to softly close. Now inhale, filling your lungs and holding it for three seconds . . . as you exhale, feel yourself letting go.

Good. Now take another deep breath . . . even deeper than before . . . hold . . . and exhale completely. Feel your entire body relaxing even more.

Take one final deep breath and . . . without letting any air out . . . take in even more air and hold. And while you're holding that breath, let your body relax even further. Now release the breath. Let it all out . . . completely empty your lungs. As you begin to breathe naturally, notice your stomach as it gently rises and falls. It's as if the entire universe were breathing through you. Imagine that all cares and worries are floating away with each exhalation.

As these gentle breaths continue, put your awareness in the middle of your chest—your heart chakra. Allow yourself to be gently rocked by the natural rhythm of your breathing.

With each inhale and exhale, visualize brilliant currents of vital life-force energy flowing in and out through your heart center. When you breathe in, imagine that you're drawing in a shimmering golden light . . . and when you exhale, watch that bright light radiating out to those you love and to the universe.

Let your body go even more. The small muscles around your eyes are utterly at ease and smooth. Your brow is relaxed and tranquil. Your jaw muscles are very slack. Your thoughts dissolve and fade away, as an inner glow envelops you. Take a deep breath in and out.

Now imagine a beautiful setting in nature. Perhaps it's somewhere you've been before or a place that exists only in your imagination. Spend some time visualizing and include specific details, making it as real as possible. If there are flowers in your sanctuary, smell and touch them. Use all of your senses to experience this place in nature. Imagine or sense that you're walking or running . . . see yourself healthy and carefree. You're breathing in the fresh, revitalizing air. Somewhere there's a clear, still body of water. Take a moment to become aware of it. It might be a spring-fed pool where you can see your own reflection—but altered, as if in a dream.

As you stand near it, you notice that a mist is rising. The spiraling mist begins to form a cloud that hugs the earth. From the center of this cloud, you're aware of a faint hum growing louder and louder. Intuitively, you realize that your master guide is approaching. The center of this swirling mist is the arrival point for this being.

Your guide has come forth to offer you love and support, and you feel this unconditional acceptance. Reach out your hand into the mist. As you do so, be aware of your guide's hand gently slipping into your own. In this moment, allow yourself to experience a relaxation so deep that it seems to touch the core of your being. The mist is beginning to disappear, and you have the opportunity to meet your master guide. It's perfectly all right if you're not able to see him or her; just get a sense or feeling of this loving being.

*Greet your guide and ask his or her name. Just
accept whatever comes forth. Spend some time talking to your spirit helper and inquire if he or she has
any special advice for you. You could ask any questions that you might have, or you may simply want
to sit with your guide. Your guide can help you in
your past-life explorations. Know that you can visit
this spiritual being whenever you want.*

Say good-bye to your guide.

*At this time, you may wish to drift off to sleep.
Whenever you want to return to normal waking consciousness, simply take a deep breath . . . and in your
own time, allow your eyes to open.*

If you do this guided meditation before going to
sleep, be sure to record what you remember the next
morning. Watch for a loving spirit to appear in your
dreams; even if that being takes different forms, the feeling emanating from it will be the same. Over time, these
recurring sensations and images will be a familiar indication of your guide's presence. Be alert and open to these
signs—otherwise, you may discount them at first. The
more you believe in and interact with your guides, the
stronger they'll grow and will become an integral part of
your life.

Spirit-Animal Guides

The use of totems (also called animal guides, power
animals, or spirit animals) in native traditions is well
documented. Members of these cultures believe that
each person has an animal spirit providing guidance and

strength. There can be more than one assisting at any time, although there's usually a single major totem that is influencing, guiding, and teaching.

Totems often appear in meditations and past-life regressions as spirit guides for those who've had previous lives in native cultures. If you've had a life in an indigenous society, it's not uncommon for you to encounter a spirit animal as your guide into your past incarnations. However, your totem may also be an indication of an alignment from a past life. For example, someone who has the cat as his or her power animal may have had a past life in Egypt; if an individual has a black panther totem, he or she may have lived in the Mayan civilization; and a panda spirit guide could indicate that a person has spent a previous lifetime in China.

Each spirit animal has its own qualities and abilities, and by communing with a particular totem, you gain access to its traits. Although the meanings attributed to certain power animals can vary according to the specific culture, there are some similarities. Oftentimes a person with the bear totem will be a good healer and have the introspection of that animal but could find it challenging to come out of the cave. Those with a deer totem may be involved with others—interrelating and interacting well—and are fertile with diverse life experiences. They may also have an adaptable nature like the deer but sometimes need protection from hunters, as some individuals may prey upon them. People with the eagle totem may see into other dimensions and have extrasensory perception, yet they often find themselves alone.

Finding Your Spirit Animal

There are a number of ways you can find your power animal. It may repeatedly appear in your dreams or during meditation, or you may recognize it by observing the animals that you're drawn to. Sometimes a personal totem is your favorite animal from childhood. Be aware that your power animal may reveal itself to you in an unusual manner. For instance, if an owl's feather drops at your feet as you walk in the woods, there's a good chance that the owl is one of your totems. If you see a particular animal again and again in different forms, it may be your totem. Perhaps you feel particularly drawn to a painting of horses; then someone sends you a photograph of a beautiful stallion; and on top of that, these magnificent animals begin to appear in your dreams—these are all signs indicating that the horse is very likely your spirit-animal guide.

Observing the attributes of particular animals is also helpful in discovering your totem. For example, bears wake up slowly and tend to be creatures of habit. So if you leap out of bed in the morning full of energy to start your day and tend to vary your activities, it's unlikely that the bear is your totem. Learning the characteristics of animals and comparing them with your personality offers valuable insights in identifying your spirit helper. Your power animal can bring an understanding of your strengths as well as assist you in times of distress. You can communicate with your totem in much the same way as you do with a guide that takes a human form.

Discovering your spirit animal creates a powerful portal into your past lives. Simply learning what your totem is and then communing with this animal while in a meditative state can allow memories of your past lives to flood into your consciousness.

The following meditation is designed to assist you in connecting with your animal guide. Like the earlier meditation, you can record yourself reading this and play it back just before you go to sleep, or you can do it with a friend who reads it aloud to you.

Meditation for Finding Your Animal Guide

Sit or lie comfortably in a quiet place and become aware of your breathing. Stop for a moment and monitor the shallowness or deepness of your breath. Then take a full, complete breath, filling your abdomen so that it expands like a balloon. Hold it and then exhale very slowly and gently. Repeat this exercise.

As your breathing becomes more rhythmic, turn your attention to the oxygen entering through your nostrils. Visualize yourself inhaling the purest, cleanest, and healthiest air. Give it a color, and observe as that hue radiates down deep inside the cavity of your lungs, oxygenating and revitalizing all the parts it reaches. Imagine that your breathing is healing and regenerating your entire body. Continue with nice, full, easy breaths. Be conscious of the air that's flowing in and out of your lungs. There's a pulse, a cadence, to the universe—at this moment, your breath is aligned with it. You are in harmony with all the patterns and rhythms of life.

Now that you're completely relaxed, you can begin an inward journey that will assist you in finding your animal guide. In your imagination, travel to a beautiful place in nature. You can picture a location that you've been to before where you've felt very comfortable, or you can travel to a setting that exists in your imagination. If you have difficulty visualizing this peaceful spot, just get a feeling of it. Feel how good it would be to find yourself in this lovely place. Get a sense of the freshness of the air and the power of the earth beneath you, and spend some time absorbing the energy of this serene area. [If you're making a recording of this meditation, you might leave a moment of silence here.]

Now find a place to sit down—it might be on a boulder, a tree stump, or a sand dune—and make yourself comfortable. Imagine that a mist is beginning to form. It becomes thicker and thicker until you can't see anything around you. As you sit, your intuition—your sixth sense—is expanding. Although you can't see it, you know that your spirit animal is approaching. You can sense the strength, wildness, and power of your totem. Now reach out into the mist and touch your animal helper. Do you feel fur, feathers, or reptilian scales? Perhaps you feel something wet, like an animal that lives in the sea? At this moment, there's an instant rapport between you and your totem. As the mist clears, you can see or feel the presence of your animal guide. You have a few moments to commune with your guide, who may speak to you or just be with you in silence and love.

When you feel complete, say good-bye to your animal guide.

Angels

History and mythology are filled with references to angels. They've inspired artists and writers as well as religious leaders. Angels may assume many forms; however, most people are familiar with them appearing as heavenly beings with wings. Almost every culture in the world has adherents of these types of angels. Native Americans called them the Bird People, and there are also accounts of benevolent winged creatures in ancient Mesopotamia and Assyria. There are angels in Christianity, Buddhism, Taoism, Judaism, Zoroastrianism, and in Islamic traditions. The Vikings named them *valkyries,* the ancient Persians called them *fereshta,* and the Greeks referred to them as *horae.* There are sightings of these divine winged spirits all over the world.

Beyond the myth, angels are real. They carry the essence of innocence and purity and are touched by the hand of the Creator. They are messengers from Spirit and are associated with higher nature, beauty, peace, fulfillment, laughter, and love. They're here to help us lay down the burdens of anxiety, uncertainty, guilt, pain, and worry; and they heal our lost faith, broken trust, and shattered innocence. They replace feelings of unworthiness and insecurity with those of happiness and belonging, enabling us to live with joy instead of fear.

Angels are different from guides in that they haven't lived an earthly existence. They are of the stars, and guides are of the Earth plane. These divine beings haven't experienced our world in a human body, so they don't have karmic or evolutionary issues to work out. There are many types of angels, from nature angels to angel messengers to your very own guardian angel—and they can each serve a different function in your life.

Guardian Angels

The most common and powerful is your guardian angel, a very special being who's been with you since the time of your birth. He or she can help you explore the unique gifts that you were born with and find ways to freely express them. (To connect with your ethereal guardian, you can use either of the previous meditations. Instead of seeking a master guide or a totem, simply focus on your desire to meet your guardian angel.)

Nature Angels

Places in nature that have a special feeling are most often under the protective shield of angels. A nature angel is a guardian or protector of a particular area. For example, an entire mountain might be under the care of this type of angel, or a lake can have an angel who watches over it.

People have shared remarkable stories about angels with me (beings both with and without wings), and each story carries a magical feeling of light and love. One woman, flying home from her vacation, decided to finish her last roll of film by taking pictures of clouds through the plane window. A few days later, she received an urgent phone call from the film processors who asked her to come down to the shop.

When she arrived, they wanted to know how she'd produced the images that appeared on the clouds. "What images?" she asked. "They're just clouds!" Then they showed her the photos. In the middle of each of the clouds was the most beautiful angel with large golden wings and a radiant smile. She stated that the angel looked like a male with short brown hair and was in very clear detail.

One man told me that in his youth he'd lived in the country, and on his family's property was a small lake. One day he took a walk by it and saw two angels flying back and forth over it. He ran to get his brother, who was 18 at the time. His brother didn't want to come, but the young boy dragged him, and when they got to the lake the angels were still floating above, apparently not noticing either of them. They sat and watched the angels for about an hour.

These stories serve as examples of nature angels, and although I can't prove their validity, both of these people were credible. Moreover, I've heard hundreds of similar stories through the years.

Archangels

Archangels, such as the Archangel Michael with his sword of truth, are other types of angels. These beings serve as guardians for our entire planet. You may also adapt the meditations in this chapter to call upon archangels and connect with them. Here's a partial list of these ethereal beings and the qualities associated with them.

- Ariel: heals and protects nature and animals, especially wild animals

- Gabriel: boosts creativity, helps with art and communication, assists in purification

- Raphael: heals physical ailments; the archangel of love, joy, and laughter

- Uriel: activates wisdom and ideas; also a healer of natural disasters

Messenger Angels

These angels will sometimes take on the human form for brief periods in order to deliver a message, offer help in time of danger, or teach an important lesson. They appear when needed and then simply disappear. These spiritual messengers seem to assume a physical form that's comforting and pleasing to the individual they're contacting. I've heard numerous reports describing these angelic beings, and I've had a number of personal experiences with them, too. (To read about angel encounters, please see my book *If I Can Forgive, So Can You.*) These spirits may be male or female, young or old, and of any race; some are well dressed and others appear in shabby garments. They all offer guidance and help in a nonintrusive way.

One man recounted a time when his truck broke down on a narrow mountain road during a winter blizzard. A part of his four-wheel drive mechanism was broken, and he was miles from any assistance. He'd just about given up hope, when a man came along in a truck who just *happened* to have the part that he needed. The stranger also helped him pull his truck out of the snow where it had gotten stuck. But when the grateful man turned to thank the individual once he got his truck started, not only were the helpful stranger and his vehicle gone, but there were no tire marks in the snow!

Again, I have no way of verifying these amazing stories, but the sheer volume of accounts of angel sightings or angelic intervention—as well my own personal experiences—gives credence to the idea that they are real and are here to help us.

Superimposed Angels

Sometimes an angel will superimpose its energy on an individual. When this occurs, a person may unwittingly offer assistance and guidance to someone—and never even remember it! It will seem as if a tremendous force of goodness momentarily takes over and provides just the right message to another person in need. Of course there can be many explanations for this, but I believe that it's most often due to angelic intervention. This phenomenon can occur for just a few seconds or for a prolonged period of time. One poignant example of this occurred many years ago in my life.

Of all my teachers, the one who will always hold a sacred place in my heart is Dancing Feather. In the strangest way, he helped me see the significance of past-life regression through his insistence on healing and forgiving the past. As he lay dying in the Santa Fe Indian Hospital, I was with him and asked, "Dancing Feather, what's the most important thing you would have me know?" With a gnarled brown finger, he beckoned me to lean in closer. "Keep it simple," he whispered softly. Then he smiled and fell back weakly against his pillow. I was expecting to hear sage, ancient Native American secrets, but that was all he said. And then slowly, like a gentle tide coming to shore, the truth sank in. I've never forgotten the wisdom of his statement. *Keep it simple!*

And then his last words to me were: "Denise, wherever you are, wherever you go . . . I'll be there."

I walked out of the hospital with a heavy heart, knowing that I'd never see my dear teacher again in this lifetime. *How could he be there? He was going to die!* I began to cry, at first slowly and softly. Then I looked up at the sky where dark, formidable clouds were forming. It had been a very dry year, and the crops were suffering from the drought. Suddenly a cool wind came up and huge drops of rain began to soak into the red, parched earth. I cried harder as shafts of lightning tore across the sky. I felt that the spirits of the sky were also grieving the loss of my teacher. I began to run.

Although my vision was blurred by the pelting rain and my own tears, I saw what I thought was an old, drunken Indian slumped over on the side of the road. As I passed him, he flung up his head as if a steel bar had been pushed up his spine, looked straight at me, and said clearly and with authority, "I won't forget." Then he slumped over again. When I heard those words, I knew that Dancing Feather would indeed "be there." It seemed that for just a moment an angel had superimposed itself on this person to make sure that I got the message from my beloved mentor.

After his death, a peculiar thing began to happen. Whenever I conducted a seminar on healing, people who had the gift of sight would say, "I see a Native American standing beside you." And they would describe my old teacher perfectly. Although I didn't see him, I knew that he was keeping his word and was with me. *"Wherever you are, wherever you go . . . I'll be there."*

How Do You Know If an Angel Is Near?

Although some people have reported seeing angels, most aren't seen but can be felt or sensed. There are several ways of telling if an angel is present. The wonderful fragrance of flowers often accompanies them; and sometimes they announce their arrival with a slight breeze, even if all the windows are closed. (This is caused by the flutter of their wings—yes, some angels do have wings!) You may hear something resembling the sound of bells, chimes, or trumpets when they're around. Oftentimes people observe bright lights, which indicates an angel's arrival. But the most common way is simply the feeling that there's an angel present . . . it's like a warm wave of love washing over you. If you sense that you're in the presence of an angel, you most likely are.

From archangels to your guardian angel, all of these compassionate beings are bridging your physical reality with their pure spiritual energy. The more that you trust and believe in them, the more they will pour their blessings upon you.

Angels have been waiting for us to be ready, and now is the time. Multitudes of angels will make their presence known in the years ahead, as we heal old wounds from the past and step into the future.

Receiving Spirit Guidance Through "Signs"

Sometimes guidance from the spirit realm comes in the form of signs. After loved ones pass on, it's not uncommon for a "sign" to appear to let everyone know that they're okay. I've heard from numerous people about their own personal experiences with this. Just before my father died, he said that if there really was a heaven, he'd put a big *M* in the sky. (He laughed when he said it because he was an atheist and believed that heaven didn't exist.) A couple of weeks after his death, I was driving a van full of my students when someone shouted, "Look, there's an *M* in the sky!" (I hadn't told them about what my father had said.) We all piled out of the vehicle and there—in the clear blue sky—was a perfect letter *M*.

Signs are also the way that our angels, ancestors, and spirit guides communicate with us. (For more information, please see my book *The Secret Language of Signs*.) Soon after Dancing Feather's death, feathers began to appear around me under remarkable circumstances; and amazingly, they also began to show up around people who attended my seminars and read my books. The reason why I'm going to tell you more about feathers as signs from Spirit is because it's very possible that you'll start experiencing this, too . . . and each time you see one, *it's likely that it will carry a message for you.*

Feathers as Signs from Spirit

In many native beliefs, feathers are thought to be the connection between humans and the spirit world. Perhaps they're sacred because they come from birds—and birds, in some cultures, are considered to be messengers between heaven and Earth. Feathers are also customarily worn on natives' headdresses because it's believed that the hollow shaft of the feather allows the Creator to communicate directly to the human being through it . . . and it also allows a person's prayers to rise up through the shaft toward the heavens. Feathers are a kind of reflection from Spirit, the same way that the light reflections of a mirrored ball are manifestations from their source.

I don't know exactly what they have to do with reincarnation, but when I was teaching courses on past lives, I'd notice their frequent appearance; sometimes, they'd even float from the ceiling of a hotel room.

A woman who had attended one of my past-life seminars—in which I'd mentioned the possibility of feathers bearing messages—wrote me this unusual story. It was only one of many such accounts.

> *I am a single mother with three young children. I was going through a very hard time in my life when I couldn't financially or emotionally take care of myself or my kids. I thought they'd be better off without me. One morning I arose with a clear decision to commit suicide. I just couldn't go on one more day. Then I heard a knock at my door. I opened it and looked to the right and the left, but no one was there. Just as I was closing the door, I gazed downward, and at my doorstep were three perfectly laid out, shiny, beautiful feathers. As I stared at them, I thought of my three beautiful children—and then I knew I was going to make it. Seeing those three feathers was a turning point for me. I'm now financially and emotionally stable and really enjoying my life and my kids.*

I've heard similar stories again and again, and each one seems to communicate a message. Sometimes it was "You're doing fine; just keep going." At other times, the message would indicate a new direction to take in life.

I believe that the feathers carry the wisdom from Spirit, and they are a fulfillment of the covenant that Dancing Feather made on his deathbed.

Many people who've read this book in the earlier edition have written to say that *feathers have started appearing in their lives!* As you begin to discover who you were in previous incarnations and resolve past-life negative programming, feathers may begin to appear to you. By doing the exercises in these chapters, you embark on an incredible journey of self-exploration, and feathers may serve as reminders that you're not alone on your voyage. There are spirit helpers around you right now, loving you and guiding you. They're helping you remember who you are by facilitating your release of old blockages.

Whenever you see a feather, be still for a moment and listen for the message. It can be a feather that you see on the ground, one that appears in your home, or even one that floats down from the sky. It can be little or large. Each one is a messenger from Spirit. I share this gift with you from my teacher—he would have liked it that way.

Calling upon Your Guides, Ancestors, and Angels for Past-Life Exploration

Before pursuing past-life exploration, it's valuable to spend a few minutes calling upon your guide, ancestor, or guardian angel. After you've spent a few minutes relaxing, visualize your spiritual helper. (You can use the guided processes earlier in this chapter to get in touch with these divine beings.)

If you can't get a visual picture of your guide, imagine or sense a large, glowing sphere of gold, white, or silver light. Feel yourself surrounded by this luminescent bubble of love and protection. After you've done this, say to yourself:

> *Dear Guardian, I ask for your assistance and guidance as I explore my past lives. Help me understand who I was and why I chose those experiences. Allow me to forgive and dissolve any personal barriers that originated in the past. I ask for your assistance to heal old emotional wounds on this past-life journey. Even if I don't consciously remember my entire voyage, I know that you're with me, helping me resolve and release the past. And I give thanks for your loving blessings.*

I've found that this invocation produces remarkable results.

As you connect with your guides or angels, you'll find it much easier to recall your past. This is because they contribute to a feeling of safety while you're exploring previous incarnations in your dreams, regressions, and in waking life. In no small way, your spirit helpers are the door keepers to your far past. The best results during regressions take place when you feel secure, and this occurs when you're tuned in to your higher guidance. These compassionate beings are so beneficial that I rarely do a past-life exploration without calling upon them for their assistance. Their loving presence helps direct the course of any inner journey.

Chapter Ten

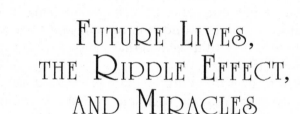

FUTURE LIVES,
THE RIPPLE EFFECT,
AND MIRACLES

As a small child, I sat forlornly on a rusty swing one foggy morning. My parents were having violent, physical arguments; and I was having a hard time coping with it all. My feet barely reached the ground as I shuffled my toes back and forth on the dirt. Suddenly I turned my head around, quickly looking behind myself. I thought I'd sensed someone approaching, but no one was there. Then I remember a deep calmness and a sense of belonging settling over me. I no longer felt alone. After that point, although I didn't like my parents' fights, I no longer felt devastated after each one as I had before. Something had changed.

This memory had been completely forgotten until some 30 years later, when I was endeavoring to go back in time during a meditation in order to visit myself as a small child. In my visualization, I popped out of a time tunnel to 1955 to find myself comforting a very young Denise as she sat slumped on a rusty swing. I told her that I loved her unconditionally. I let her know that she had some tough times ahead, but she would make it and her future would be wonderful. As I spoke to her, she straightened up and it seemed that a heavy weight had been lifted from her spirit.

Coming back into the present time, I was astonished. Not only had I traveled back and visited my younger self—which of course anyone can practice doing—but the amazing thing was that as a small child in 1955, *I remembered* the visit! I don't recall someone talking to me that foggy morning, but I do remember sensing that someone who cared for me was by my side. And even though I couldn't see who it was, I knew that I didn't need to feel lonely anymore. It was a remarkable experience—I know that I *indeed* visited myself, and it had made an enormous difference in my life.

I also believe that not only can you visit your younger self to provide solace and love, but you can also call upon your spirit beyond the present to bring advice and guidance based on what you've learned in the future.

One of the many objections to this theory is the idea that time is fixed and can't be altered. However, time isn't an absolute. It's an infinite eternity, arbitrarily divided into portions called centuries, years, months, weeks, days, hours, seconds, and so on. In the past, we thought of time as steady and unchanging. I believe that the more you explore the universes within yourself—through meditation or other spiritual practices—the more fluid the passage of time becomes. You can actually perceive it speeding up or slowing down.

Time as a Product of Perception

Time is a product of your awareness; the only *time* that actually exists is what you perceive. When you're involved in something creative, *time flies* and an hour seems like a blink of an eye. By contrast, when you're waiting for a friend who's an hour late, time seems to stretch for an eternity.

You can speed it up or slow it down subjectively. This is what I call entering *hyper-time,* an expression I coined because it most accurately describes this phenomenon. *Merriam-Webster's Collegiate Dictionary* defines the prefix *hyper* as "that is or exists in a space of more than three dimensions." Entering hyper-time is literally stepping into "time that dwells beyond the three dimensions." In my reincarnation seminars, I teach participants how to access this realm. Using powerful breathing and movement techniques, I've developed methods to *snap-shift* perceptual reality in order to shift a person's perception of time.

I've heard remarkable stories from seminar participants who've integrated these techniques into their lives. One woman shared the following story with me: For 18 years, she'd worked at the same job. To get there, she always drove the same route at the same speed, and there usually wasn't much variation in traffic conditions. It almost always took her exactly 47 minutes to travel from home to work. She told me that after participating in my seminar, she decided to test the methods that I'd taught. She entered hyper-time before she left for work but otherwise did everything exactly the same as always, yet she got to work in 32 minutes! This isn't an unusual story. Many participants of my seminars have reported similar events in their lives.

Given the current laws that govern our physical world, it should be impossible to alter minutes and seconds in such a manner. But what if time really is fluid? What if it contracts and expands in a rhythmically pulsating universe? What if time is a function of our perception? Imagine that we can dramatically shift it and enter into the timeless Source from which all awareness emanates. Suppose we could travel to dimensionless regions where time and space are born? Given these suppositions, we could in fact alter time and even our view of reality. I believe that these notions *are* true and that each and every one of us is both the perceiver and definer of *time.*

Reality by Agreement

I believe that our view of reality is created *by agreement,* and our understanding of the past is also determined in this manner. If many people agree on something, then it becomes a reality. For example, lots of people concur that Picasso was a great painter; thus, Picasso was a great painter because people agree on the value of his art. If no one had ever accepted this, then Picasso wouldn't be considered a great painter.

I also believe that form, too, coalesces around our collective beliefs and agreements. For instance, the world used to be flat. During a certain time in our history, everyone agreed with this statement, and all the evidence available supported this view. Now the world is round. Science proves that this is so—in fact, it proves that the world was *always* round. If, in the future, it was revealed that the earth is actually a hologram projected from another universe, all the evidence would support this fact—and that the earth had indeed always been a hologram.

We're constantly changing not just our present, but our past and our future as well from any given point in time. The universe is a fluctuating ocean of consciousness with all time occurring simultaneously. We're intimately connected in this sea of awareness. When you release an old blockage through changing your perception of the past, it's like a pebble dropped in a still pool whose ripples are felt at the farthest shore. Not only does it help you, but your immediate family members and friends are also affected positively by the "ripples," and so is everyone else on the planet who shares your frequencies . . . even if they don't know you.

The Ripple Effect

Here's an example of how the ripple effect works: Daniel came to me for assistance because he was having money problems. He'd invest time and effort into a project, but his financial gain would be disproportionately small. Daniel was very discouraged and felt that there must be some inner blockage causing the problem. He regressed to a life in the Middle East in which he was a merchant (he is of Middle Eastern descent in this life).

In his past life, he discovered that he wasn't always fair in his financial practices with others. During Daniel's regression, he recalled a traumatic event that was motivated by his business interactions in that life.

> It was a searing day, the heat permeating every corner and fold of life. Although the darkness of the merchant's home offered some respite from the heat, the lengthening shadows of the approaching evening were welcome. The merchant looked lovingly at his young son, who had just come in from outside.
>
> Suddenly the merchant felt a presence in the doorway. A man towered over him, an individual the merchant knew only slightly. In an instant, however, the merchant understood why the man was there. Recently, the merchant had unfairly gotten the better of him in a business transaction.
>
> Seemingly in slow motion, the man in the doorway raised a dagger high above his head and rushed forward. In one silken movement, he slit the throat of the merchant's son . . . and then fled.

The scene was so distressing that Daniel immediately came out of his regression. I said, "As painful as it seems, you can go back into that scene and change it. Turn this negative event into a positive one. Doing this will have a powerful effect on your challenges with money in your present life."

Reluctantly, he returned to the past life and replayed the scene until the man in the doorway held the knife high overhead. He then imagined the man dropping the knife and running away.

I said, "Go forward in your life as a merchant."

He then saw himself treating people fairly instead of cheating them. He imagined his reputation as a man of honor spreading throughout the land, and he visualized himself growing old and becoming more prosperous with each passing year. He watched his son grow up to become a fine young man and an honorable merchant like his father.

As a result of exploring and changing his past-life memories, two things occurred. First, Daniel's business immediately began to turn around and he's now very prosperous. He owns numerous companies and homes and travels first-class around the world. The second event was extraordinary: In Daniel's regression, he saw that his teenage son in his present life was also the son who was killed in his Middle Eastern life. In this lifetime, his son had a constant sore throat that began when he was a small boy (which was most likely due to the unresolved trauma from having died from a slit throat).

The moment when Daniel changed his past life, his son's persistent throat ailment went away, and it hasn't returned after more than 20 years. This is particularly interesting in light of the fact that Daniel had never told his family about the regression because he thought they wouldn't understand this kind of therapy.

When Daniel changed the past and released an old blockage, it had an empowering ripple effect on those around him . . . even though they didn't know what he'd done. This ripple effect influences not only those around you, but everyone else on the same frequency. It could be that—following Daniel's regression—halfway around the world, there was another individual who shared his frequency and was also struggling with finances. The next morning, the individual could have woken up feeling that a heavy burden had been lifted without ever knowing why. *We're connected.* When one is uplifted, we all are.

I'm often asked whether we could influence others negatively if we make a mistake when we change the past, but I've never seen this occur. I believe that there is a divine guiding force in life, ensuring that when you alter past events during regressions, they only bring benefits to everyone.

When you transform negative aspects, clarity and balance radiate out from you through unseen pathways, creating an enormous difference in the world around you . . . and beyond. To heal your past is an act of power, rippling out from you and touching others in ways that surpass your greatest expectations. Mother Teresa said: "It's not how much we do, but how much love we put in the doing. It's not how much we give, but how much love we put in the giving." When you put love and grace into healing your past, you'll make a tremendous difference!

Future Lives

Some people find it valuable to visit their upcoming lives or have their future selves come back through time and space in order to offer advice and guidance based on the knowledge they've gained. This is also an excellent way to assist your ability to manifest your dreams by projecting what you desire into the future. Because the time/space veil is thinning, it's becoming easier to travel in your meditations not only to the past but also to approaching events. Some people find that their inner confidence is renewed after they've witnessed destined triumphs that have yet to be realized. Others discover that they can avoid a difficult future by observing possibilities that haven't yet unfolded and making corrections today.

Sometimes individuals are concerned with how they'll cope if they see something truly terrible in their future or in a loved one's destiny. Tomorrow is as malleable as the past, and what you see is only a probability—and fortunately, you're in a position to make alterations.

The process used to travel to future lives is similar to what's used to access past lives. The following meditation will help you get started.

Future-Life Meditation

First allow yourself to become very relaxed, and picture a favorite place in nature. You might imagine yourself leaning against a willow tree as you listen to a bubbling stream nearby. Allow your entire body to become calm as you fill each and every part of yourself with tranquility. Know that every breath is enabling you to become even more comfortable. Imagine that your guide or angel is close at hand. You're at peace with the universe and are surrounded in infinite love.

Imagine that you're engulfed in a sphere of white light. You're safe and protected. As you're sitting in nature, day turns to night. One by one the stars come out, and the entire sky becomes filled with shimmering lights. A particular star draws your attention. As you gaze at it, it becomes brighter and brighter and slowly begins to float down from the sky, moving toward you.

As the star grows closer, you can see that it's actually an orb-shaped vehicle made of light and sound. It looks like a large, luminous bubble. You know this is a time machine.

You step inside and feel comforted by the lush, cocoonlike interior. Quietly, with only the softest hum, the vehicle lifts from the earth and begins to gently ascend. As you settle back into the inviting cushions, you observe the entire canopy of stars through the windows.

You feel the vehicle floating back to the earth. As you step out of your time machine, you find yourself by a beautiful, still pool. As you gaze into it, you begin to have visions. You see who you are in a future life. Notice whether you're a male or female and if any people look similar to your present-day friends or family members. Scan your future life and look for the area of greatest conflict. You're free to change the scene you're observing. In addition, see if there's anything in your present life that you can do to avert this future scenario. Surround the entire scene with love, and return to your time machine.

Begin to bring yourself to normal waking consciousness. You understand that all you've seen of your future was for your highest good, and you know that you're making the necessary adjustments in your present life in order to create an exciting, fulfilling future.

Creating Miracles

The dictionary defines a miracle as an event or action that's "totally amazing, extraordinary, or unexpected." By their very nature, miracles seem elusive and rare, yet it's possible for your life to be filled with more and more of these "extraordinary" events. In this book, I've talked about the importance of releasing blockages from the past, which will create amazing events in the future. This is the most vital step in order for miracles to blossom. If you have a deep inner barrier—no matter how much visualizing, praying, or affirming you do—you won't be able to achieve your dreams. With the information I've shared in these chapters, you've learned powerful techniques for resolving personal limitations. But once the blockages have been cleared, how do you go about creating those miracles in your life? Here are some simple yet highly effective techniques you can do to start the process.

1. Get clear on what you want. In order to achieve your dreams, you must first become clear on exactly what you desire. Wishing for a miracle without knowing exactly what you would like it to be is like taking a trip without a map and hoping that you arrive at a great location. To gain clarity, write down what you'd like your life to be like in 1 year, 2 years, 5 years, 10 years, and finally, 20 years. Make it very specific. (You can always adjust it as time goes on.)

A number of years ago, a survey was conducted at a prestigious university in which the graduating class members were asked about their personal dreams for the future. Some people had set goals and created plans to fulfill them . . . and others didn't. They interviewed the same individuals 20 years later and found that those who had specific dreams (and a plan) were not only immensely more successful, but were also much happier (by their own declaration) than those who didn't have specific dreams and a plan for fulfillment. To get where you want to go, you must first know where you are going.

To make sure that what you've written down is *really* what your soul desires, visualize all of your desired outcomes—for the future years—having come true. And then, while in that meditative state, ask yourself, *Is this really what my soul desires?*

The reason why it's important to ask this question is because often what we *consciously* want (the new house, the promotion, and so on) is at odds with what our soul yearns for (more time to relax, more time with the kids, and so forth). Make sure that what you say you want is actually what your higher self desires . . . otherwise, achieving your dreams will never bring you joy.

2. Embrace appreciation and gratitude. What you resist persists, and if you constantly resist what you have in your life, you actually energize it . . . and as strange as it may sound, you actually get more of it. In other words, you'll receive more of what you *don't* want. If you wake up—and live each day—with gratitude about who you are and what you have, it's so much easier to have miracles in your life. In fact, the more that you're thankful for what you have, the more bounty you will reap. The more angry, depressed, or sad you are about what you possess, the more scarcity and deprivation you will harvest.

3. Ask yourself, *How would it make me feel?* When someone lists all the things they want in life, it almost always isn't actually about the *things* they want, but the *feeling* that they believe those things will bring them. For example, of course you need transportation in modern life; however, if it were solely a matter of transportation just about any car would suffice. For most people, their car is more about the *feeling* that it gives them, rather than the fact that it can take them from one place to another. In other words, one person may equate a new car with a sense of freedom; and for others, it might evoke feelings such as power, sexiness, sophistication, or prosperity. But in almost every case, an individual will buy a new car because of the *feeling* they hope it will give them when they drive it.

Most people believe that achieving their heart's desire will activate particular pleasurable emotional states. But here's the secret: *If you create the feeling first, it's much easier to manifest your wishes.* Look at your list of what you want to achieve, and then ask yourself how attaining those objects or experiences is going to make you feel. Then imagine that you're actually *feeling* those emotions. If you do this consistently, very soon you'll actually experience the freedom, joy, power, confidence, and so on, that you thought your desired wish would bring you. Once you can activate the feeling, it's just an easy step to manifest your heart's desire.

4. Act "as if." Another secret to creating miracles in your life is to act *as if* they've already happened. So if you want more confidence in life, behave as if you already have it. If you want to be more abundant, act like you already are. Perhaps you've heard the expression "You have to feel it to believe it!" This is so true—the more that you can feel as if you already have your miracles, the more likely they are to happen. In this stage, you can write in your journal *as if* you were writing one year in the future. Recall all the great things that happened and most of all feel the excitement and joy, as if those things actually did happen. This is a simple yet powerful exercise . . . that really does work!

5. Take action. Without action, a dream is just a dream. It's not enough to release blockages and become clear on your goals; you must also take action. To do this, outline the steps it will take for your miracles to come to fruition . . . and then schedule time into your daily planner to make sure it happens.

6. Let it go. Sometimes we get so attached to the way we think our dream needs to unfold that we close doors that otherwise might offer opportunities. After completing the previous steps, let go of your expectations about how and when miracles will occur for you. Open your heart to your soul and to the Creator with the knowledge that your life is evolving exactly as it should for your highest growth.

7. Have faith. If you planted seeds one day, you wouldn't go out the next morning and start shouting at them because they hadn't borne fruit overnight. *Where's my fruit!* Of course you wouldn't. You'd have faith that with nurturing and care, the seeds would eventually sprout, branch, and flower. Then the fruit would ripen.

When you have a dream, do all of the preceding steps and have faith that it will happen. Don't give up two minutes before the miracle . . . and for heaven's sake, *don't dig up those seeds.*

AFTERWORD

Time, Space, and Beyond:
The Next Step

My near-death experience led me on a quest for self-understanding and to find my way back *home*. After I returned to my body, I intuitively knew there was a way to seek the Light without dying; there was a way to *be home* and still exist in a physical body. I realized there were countless dimensions coexisting with our reality, and we could be aware of them by adjusting an *inner dial.* Just as there are numerous radio stations flooding your home or office—but you can't hear them unless you have your radio on—we need only to find our inner dial, turn it on, and tune in; then we'll touch the Light.

Most people think of *heaven* as the place you go to when you die. We subconsciously think of it as somewhere way up above the clouds, but heaven, or our spiritual home, isn't in the sky. It's here, right now—a dimension coexisting with our physical reality. One way you can know that you're close to that dimension is through synchronicity. For example, when you think of something and it happens, you need something and it suddenly appears, or you think of someone and he or she calls. When I was in the Light right after being shot, there was no time between thought and creation. My thoughts were instantly manifest. The closer you get to that dimension, the faster your thoughts become manifest in the physical world.

There's nothing out there that isn't you. Because of the linear way that we perceive reality, I don't think we can ever understand this intellectually, communicate it verbally, or even write about it in a comprehensive way. However, I believe that deep inside, *we all do know this* and we've all had glimpses of this feeling. Even in the most fulfilled human being, there's a longing, a yearning, and a remembering of that exquisite place of oneness and unity.

Each and every part of the universe is a part of you, and you're the most astonishing blend imaginable. But most of us have forgotten because we usually identify only with our bodies and feel separate from all the other parts of ourselves. Sometimes we identify with our children or even our possessions (a man will run into a burning building to rescue valuables because in that moment, he's identifying himself more with his material possessions than with his body). In fact, you're living in a miraculous ocean of energy, and each part of that powerful flow is you. You might imagine all these parts as making up a gigantic orchestra of energy. When there's a harmonization of all these aspects, a vibration is created that resonates throughout the universe.

This is what my Native American ancestors meant when they talked about being in "right relation" with all things. It means to honor and respect the livingness in all things. Cherish the animal or plant that gives you life

. . . revere all that's around you. Listen—really listen—
and acknowledge the reality of your neighbors, for they
aren't separate from you. They *are* you!

Living in right relation with all things means living in harmony with all other elements of the collective
Spirit. One way to do so is to unconditionally accept the
reality of others. This also means moving toward acceptance of all parts of yourself, especially the aspects that
you've judged negatively and even what you embodied
in your past lives. Being in right relation signifies helping
others wherever you can without expecting anything in
return. It implies acting with compassion toward all the
life force.

Know that there's no less energy in your computer
than in the beautiful apple tree growing outside your
window. Honor, accept, and love the life that's all
around you, for it's all *you* in different forms. Whatever
you judge sets you further along the path of separate-
ness; whatever you love allows the orchestra of all your
parts (which in its totality is the Creator) to vibrate and
sing with joy throughout the universe. As the shackles of
the past loosen their hold, may you find true peace. May
miracles abound in your life . . . beyond your greatest
expectations!

ACKNOWLEDGMENTS

As always, I'm deeply grateful to Jill Kramer for her gracious role as my editor—I'm so blessed—and to Lisa Mitchell for her kind support of the manuscript. Much appreciation goes to the radiant Priya Kroeger for holding down the fort while I typed and for her perseverance in debating small points in the book (which really weren't small points in the end). And thanks to Diane Goodwin for her flash typing skills.

Heaps of gratitude go to Roberta Grace, Donna Abate, LuAnn Cibik, and Allison Harter—the divas of the Internet. My life is so full because you are all in it! And all my love to Colette Baron-Reid; Marika Borg; Tom Brady; Amber Dotts; Heather, Brand, and Gordon Fortner; Lynne Franks; Tamara Frey; Diana James; Debbie Kaminski; and webmaster and friend extraordinaire Louis Zimmerman for designing the beautiful cover on this book. My deep appreciation to the remarkable folks at Hay House Radio; and to Kurt, Ute, and the great folks at Primavera.

And a huge thanks to all the professional Soul Coaches and Past Life Regression Therapists whom I've trained over the years. You'll always reside in my heart with immense love.

ABOUT THE AUTHOR

Denise Linn, the best-selling author of 17 books, including *Sacred Space* and *Soul Coaching,* is an international lecturer, a healer, and a popular radio talk-show host. She is the founder of the International Institute of Soul Coaching®, a professional certification course, as well as the founder of Interior Alignment®. Denise holds seminars on five continents and appears on television and radio programs throughout the world.

Website: **www.DeniseLinn.com**

Hay House Titles of Related Interest

YOU CAN HEAL YOUR LIFE, the movie,
starring Louise Hay & Friends
(available as a 1-DVD program and an expanded 2-DVD set)
Watch the trailer at **www.LouiseHayMovie.com**

THE SHIFT, the movie,
starring Dr. Wayne W. Dyer
(available as a 1-DVD program and an expanded 2-DVD set)
Watch the trailer at **www.DyerMovie.com**

✢

ARCHANGELS & ASCENDED MASTERS: *A Guide to Working and Healing with Divinities and Deities,* by Doreen Virtue

CHANGE YOUR THOUGHTS—CHANGE YOUR LIFE: *Living the Wisdom of the Tao,* by Dr. Wayne W. Dyer

MIRRORS OF TIME: *Using Regression for Physical, Emotional, and Spiritual Healing,* by Brian L. Weiss, M.D. (book-with-CD)

POWER OF THE SOUL: *Inside Wisdom for an Outside World,* by John Holland

REMEMBERING THE FUTURE: *The Path to Recovering Intuition,* by Colette Baron-Reid

SOUL LESSONS AND SOUL PURPOSE: *A Channeled Guide to Why You Are Here,* by Sonia Choquette

THE TIMES OF OUR LIVES: *Extraordinary True Stories of Synchronicity, Destiny, Meaning, and Purpose,* by Louise Hay & Friends

TRANSFORMING FATE INTO DESTINY: *A New Dialogue with Your Soul,* by Robert Ohotto

THE UNBELIEVABLE TRUTH: *A Medium's Guide to the Spirit World,* by Gordon Smith

✢

All of the above are available at your local bookstore,
or may be ordered by contacting Hay House (see next page).

We hope you enjoyed this Hay House book.
If you'd like to receive our online catalog featuring additional
information on Hay House books and products, or if you'd like to
find out more about the Hay Foundation, please contact:

Hay House, Inc.
P.O. Box 5100
Carlsbad, CA 92018-5100

(760) 431-7695 or **(800) 654-5126**
(760) 431-6948 (fax) or **(800) 650-5115 (fax)**
www.hayhouse.com® • **www.hayfoundation.org**

Published and distributed in Australia by: Hay House Australia Pty.
Ltd., 18/36 Ralph St., Alexandria NSW 2015 • *Phone:* 612-9669-4299
Fax: 612-9669-4144 • www.hayhouse.com.au

Published and distributed in the United Kingdom by: Hay House
UK, Ltd., Astley House, 33 Notting Hill Gate, London W11 3JQ
Phone: 44-20-3675-2450 • *Fax:* 44-20-3675-2451
www.hayhouse.co.uk

Published and distributed in the Republic of South Africa by:
Hay House SA (Pty), Ltd., P.O. Box 990, Witkoppen 2068 • *Phone/Fax:*
27-11-467-8904 • info@hayhouse.co.za • www.hayhouse.co.za

Published in India by: Hay House Publishers India, Muskaan Complex, Plot No. 3, B-2, Vasant Kunj, New Delhi 110 070 • *Phone:* 91-11-
4176-1620 • *Fax:* 91-11-4176-1630 • www.hayhouse.co.in

Distributed in Canada by: Raincoast Books,
2440 Viking Way, Richmond, B.C. V6V 1N2
Phone: 1-800-663-5714 • *Fax:* 1-800-565-3770 • www.raincoast.com

---

Take Your Soul on a Vacation

Visit **www.HealYourLife.com®** to regroup, recharge,
and reconnect with your own magnificence. Featuring blogs,
mind-body-spirit news, and life-changing wisdom
from Louise Hay and friends.

Visit **www.HealYourLife.com** today!

CPSIA information can be obtained
at www.ICGtesting.com
Printed in the USA
LVOW03s0113120318
569503LV00001B/43/P

9 781401 916824